THE BROTHERS GRIMM

*Jacob and Wilhelm, as they appeared on the title page
of the* German Dictionary *in 1854*

THE BROTHERS GRIMM

Two Lives, One Legacy

BY DONALD R. HETTINGA

CLARION BOOKS ◆ NEW YORK

Thank you to the Ezra Jack Keats Foundation,
the de Grummond Children's Literature Collection
of the University of Southern Mississippi,
and the Calvin College Alumni Association
for support of the research for this book.

Clarion Books
a Houghton Mifflin Company imprint
215 Park Avenue South, New York, NY 10003
Copyright © 2001 by Donald R. Hettinga

The text was set in 14-point Cochin.
Book design by Trish Parcell Watts

LIBRARY OF CONGRESS CATALOGING-IN-PUBLICATION DATA
Hettinga, Donald R., 1953—
The Brothers Grimm : two lives, one legacy / by Donald R. Hettinga.
    p. cm.
Includes bibliographical references.
    ISBN 0-618-05599-1
    1. Grimm, Jacob, 1785–1863—Juvenile literature. 2. Grimm, Wilhelm, 1786–1859—
Juvenile literature. 3. Philologists—Germany—Biography. 4. Kinder- und Hausmèrchen.
[1. Grimm, Jacob, 1785–1863. 2. Grimm, Wilhelm, 1786–1859. 3. Philologists.] I. Title.

PD63.H48 2001
430'.92'243—dc21

                                                              00-065598
                    CRW 10 9 8 7 6 5 4 3 2 1

To Gary D. Schmidt, my hedgemaster

CONTENTS

Once Upon a Time

Once upon a time, a very real time — in fact, a time when George Washington was still General Washington and was just thinking about becoming the first president of the United States — two brothers were born in what is now Germany. Although they would become famous for many things, they would be best known for the words that begin this page: "Once upon a time." Throughout their lives these brothers, Jacob and Wilhelm Grimm, worked for kings and emperors, invented new ways of understanding language, and created the first modern German dictionary. We remember them mainly, however, for the fairy tales that they collected — for Snow White and Cinderella, Tom Thumb and Red Riding Hood, Rapunzel and Rumpelstiltskin.

These stories existed long before the Brothers Grimm. Fairy tales are part of an oral tradition that is as old as human civilization. For example, ever since its first appearance in China sometime before recorded history, the story of Cinderella has been told around fires and at bedsides on every continent. Her slipper isn't always glass and her coach isn't always made from a pumpkin. Instead, her clothes and her carriage change according to the culture in which she appears. In Egypt, her slippers are red leather and in the West Indies, the pumpkin is replaced by a breadfruit.

As with all folk- and fairy tales, the storyteller watches the audience for signs of restlessness and adapts the story to keep them listening. The Brothers Grimm are like that storyteller, and we are like the listeners enthralled by the tale. For much of their lives the brothers listened to other storytellers and scoured old books for folktales that they could write down for future generations. They believed that folktales and songs were national treasures that were in danger of being lost because fewer and fewer people remembered them. But in gathering their collection of *Hausmärchen*—household fairy tales—they created a treasure for more people than they could have imagined, for the tales, as the Brothers Grimm retold them, became more famous than those told by anyone else, forever stamping their names and the words "Once upon a time" in hearts and minds all over the world.

It is their story that you'll find in this book, the story of two brothers who grew up almost like twins. Their bond was so remarkable that they spent most of their lives together. As young boys, they shared a room and studied and played together. Sent away to school and, later, university, they roomed together. In fact, for most of their lives, the brothers worked and lived together.

Even after Wilhelm was married, Jacob lived with him and his wife. Wilhelm's son Herman would later say that "the brothers had one house, one library, one purse."

If their story is a story of friendship, it is also a story of courage and hard work. They had to struggle against poverty and sickness. They had to watch as foreign soldiers captured their city. They had to face persecution when they stood up for what they believed. They had to deal with sorrow as people they dearly loved died.

But with their struggles came much joy. They became friends with many of the great writers and artists of the German kingdoms, where they lived all their lives. They worked beside kings in peace and in war. They became national heroes and gained the respect of writers and scholars all over the world.

At the celebration of what would have been Jacob's one hundredth birthday, a German scholar said that while "great learning" quite often "leads to pride, self-satisfaction, [and] jealousy," that didn't happen in the case of Jacob and Wilhelm. Instead, at the top "of their life and fame they remained simple, good men," who "sympathized with children, as well as with the wordly-wise, with statesmen, and poets."

CHAPTER ONE

A Fairy Tale Childhood

Once upon a time there was a husband and a wife who for quite some time had been wishing in vain for a child. Finally, the Lord gave the wife a sign of hope that their wish would be fulfilled.

— RAPUNZEL

When Jacob Ludwig Carl Grimm was born on January 4, 1785, his parents, Philipp and Dorothea, couldn't have received a better holiday present. The year before, their firstborn son, Friedrich, had died when he was only a few months old—as many children did in those days. And so, they were happy that Jacob grew to be a healthy one-year-old and that, the next year, they had another son, born February 24, 1786. They named him Wilhelm Carl Grimm.

The brothers shared more than just a middle name. As they were growing up, they shared just about everything. Although they later had three more brothers—Carl, Ferdinand, and Ludwig (and another two who died as infants)—and a sister,

Dorothea Grimm

Philipp Grimm

Charlotte—they had a special connection with each other that set them apart from the rest of the family.

In many ways, their early years were typical of what we now call a middle-class childhood. In the beginning of the eighteenth century, families were either nobles or peasants, but in the latter half of the century, people who worked as merchants or lawyers or clergymen became increasingly important in their communities. Since Philipp Grimm was a lawyer and the town clerk of Hanau in Hesse, the kingdom in which they were born, the brothers lived quite comfortably during the first few years of their lives.

The family had two servants—Gretchen, a nurserymaid, who told the boys stories and sneaked them treats of bread and cheese on the attic stairs, and Marie, who helped their mother with cooking and with cleaning the house. As in most families like theirs, the servants took care of the children while the father attended to business and the mother supervised the household and spent a lot of time sewing and knitting clothes for the family. Once a week a washerwoman would come to wash their clothes in steaming tubs in the house's narrow courtyard. Sometimes she would pour a drop of brandy on a piece of brown bread for each of the boys as a treat.

The house was a big, mysterious place to Jacob and Wilhelm. Their father's study, its walls covered with law books, was mostly off-limits, but from its upstairs window they could look out over the courtyard and spy into the fruit trees in the neighbors' gardens. The downstairs drawing room was another place they were supposed to stay out of. But the boys were fascinated by the wallpaper pattern of brown and green huntsmen adventuring out over a background the color of snow. (Wallpaper was something of a luxury at the time; most people of the village lived in houses whose rooms had painted walls.) And sometimes in the winter, the boys would sneak into the room to press hot coins against the frost-covered windows, making circle designs in the ice.

The family probably spent the most time together in the main living room, a comfortable room with green wallpaper. This was where the family ate, around a table with a red-and-black-spotted oilcloth; where they gathered together in the evening for reading or for prayers; and where, in the corner by the warm stove, the brothers would take baths—in a washtub filled with warm water and wine! (Jacob said that it smelled sweet but stung his eyes.)

This was where Jacob and Wilhelm knelt before their mother while she picked lice from their hair, a ritual that, surprisingly, the brothers enjoyed.

The brothers were discouraged from playing with the other children of the town, so they spent most of their time together, sometimes under the eye (*and* hands *and* feet) of Gretchen and Marie, sometimes under the eye of their aunt. Tante Schlemmer was their father's older sister and would later come to live with them. She was the boys' first teacher.

Considerably older than their father, Julianne Schlemmer was a stern woman with high expectations of the boys, especially of Jacob, who, she thought, looked like her grandfather, Friedrich Grimm. He had been an important minister in the region. He was the chaplain to the Prince of Isenburg and the inspector of churches around Hanau. In fact, he had written the version of the catechism—the lessons about God and the church—that all Protestant children in the region studied. His son, also named Friedrich, had been a minister as well, and for many years the Grimms, especially Tante Schlemmer, perhaps because Philipp had chosen the law instead of the church, assumed that Jacob, as the oldest son, would carry on the tradition. Jacob must have thought so, too, because he would sometimes stand on a stool and preach, imitating his grandfather.

Tante Schlemmer told the boys stories from the Bible and drilled them in reading and writing. They read from a little book that had a picture of children blowing bubbles on its wooden front cover and a picture of a red cornet on the back. Using an ivory rib from a broken fan, their aunt would point to the letters again and again as the boys learned the alphabet and some simple words.

Later, when Jacob kept mixing up his *p*'s and his *q*'s, she used a long pin to point at the letters, and after a time all the pages of their reader were filled with tiny holes from her energetic teaching.

But if Philipp Grimm wanted his sons to know the Bible and to mind their *p*'s and *q*'s, he also wanted them to be able to mix with the people of the upper classes. So after they learned to read, Jacob and Wilhelm—young as they were—studied dancing and French with a tutor. On the days that they had these lessons they would set out hand in hand down the street, sometimes tempted to stop at the glovemaker's shop across the way for a leather ball or other scraps to play with, sometimes tempted to daydream and watch the golden weathercock on top of the church turning in the wind.

Soon, however, they had to say good-bye to the weathercock and the glovemaker and all the familiar people and sights of Hanau. Their father had been made *Amtmann*, or magistrate, in the nearby town of Steinau. So in 1791, the Grimms—now with Jacob (six), Wilhelm (five), Carl (four), Ferdinand (three), and Ludwig (one)—wrapped their chairs and glassware in straw and piled into a small carriage for the ride to the town that would become their home. Wilhelm sat on a yellow tin box or slept on his aunt's lap. He couldn't believe that the blossoms on the thorn trees that lined the road were really flowers. Until the driver broke off a branch for him, he thought that the black branches were covered with snow.

Their new house, the *Amtshaus*, represented both their new status—the Amtmann was an important man in the community— and the new adventures they would have. It was a large, old house, with a turret to spy from and thick stone walls that had

ABOVE: *The Amtshaus, in a watercolor painting by Ludwig Emil Grimm*

OPPOSITE
TOP: *The Amtshaus looks much the same today as it did in 1800.*
LEFT: *The brothers were fascinated by the carvings on the beams of the Amtshaus.*
RIGHT: *The stone posts in the courtyard of the Amtshaus show the effects of hundreds of years of weathering.*

already withstood more than two hundred years of weather. A stone wall more than six feet tall surrounded the courtyard and gardens. There was a barn across from the house, and stables connected to a wing of the house. The boys loved the huge lime tree that stood in front of the door and was as high as the roof.

But what they liked best of all were the things that made the house magical: the lucky storks that had built a nest on a tower next to the house; the faces and figures—even the slightly scary squinting devils—that were carved into the ends of the beams and rafters; the coachman, who wore a special uniform and who would playfully lift them up on the horses but who would also very seriously serve them as a butler at dinner; the stream that flowed just behind the house on the other side of the wall; the sledge, with a golden Hessian lion on its side, that they'd ride in on winter outings; the stories that neighbors told about the ghost of a former Amtmann that haunted their very house!

The brothers soon settled into the routine of daily life. The day began with the sounds of their father getting up. Jacob and Wilhelm would lie in bed, looking at the green-and-white-striped wallpaper and picturing what was happening in the sitting room just beyond them. When they heard the tea urn start up, they knew that their father was next door in his cotton nightshirt, reading prayers for the day. Shortly after, the aroma of his pipe would waft through the house, and the coachman-butler would help Herr Grimm with his hair, putting it into a fashionable pigtail and powdering it. After breakfast would come their lessons.

During their first few years in Steinau, Jacob and Wilhelm still didn't go to school. Instead, their teacher came to them, teaching them in a special schoolroom in the house from ten or eleven

The stones in the courtyard of the Amtshaus where the brothers played

The courtyard of the castle in Steinau

o'clock until noon and from two to three o'clock in the afternoon. Herr Zinckhan was not to be the boys' favorite teacher. He had been a teacher since 1777, and the brothers thought that his teaching, as well as his wig and clothing, was long out of date. Jacob, in particular, who had been able to read whole articles in the newspaper since he was five, was bored by the strict old teacher's drills in reading and grammar.

If Jacob and Wilhelm's lessons were anything like Ludwig's when he studied under Herr Zinckhan a few years later, it's not surprising that the boys were bored. Their youngest brother, who, unlike Jacob and Wilhelm, had class in a schoolhouse in town, said that Herr Zinckhan would line the boys up to check if they had their books with them. Anyone without a grammar book was given a beating and sent home to get it. Then, at the start of each day's lesson, Herr Zinckhan would ask the boys the same questions:

"What is a Latin grammar?"
   "It is an explanation of the Latin language, sir, teaching the correct way of writing, understanding, and speaking."

Then another pupil would be asked, "What is a Greek grammar?" and a third, "What is a Hebrew grammar? A Hungarian?" and so on, the answer being the same each time. After asking the boys some vocabulary words in Latin or French, Herr Zinckhan would tell them to sit down and learn their words better, and then he would turn to other tasks—like putting a new string on his violin or fitting a new wick in a lamp.

While lessons were boring for Jacob and Wilhelm, little else in

Herr Johann Georg Zinckhan, the brothers' teacher in Steinau

A view of the town square of Steinau from the castle

Steinau was. The household was filled with interesting things to do and watch. Jacob was intrigued by the butchering in the courtyard and his mother's sausage making in the kitchen. There were stone steps to jump down and servants to spy on. There was medicine to mix with honey for the animals, and there were all sorts of animals to watch and feed: chickens, ducks, pigeons, horses, cows, and — a favorite — the lambkins. There was the little hut in the courtyard to play in; once Jacob took a bath in its tub and ran naked through the yard. He was grateful for the yard's high walls.

The world beyond those walls was also intriguing. Jacob and

Wilhelm loved to spend time exploring the city and the country-side. Some days they would play in the center of town near the moat of the castle that was just two blocks from their house. Other days they would play behind their house, along the banks of the Stadtborn, making waterwheels and boats out of twigs and leaves or sketching houses or people. And there were always interesting things to watch: potters toting clay, tanners carrying hides, woods-men carting loads of logs, the goose girl driving her flock, or cows wandering home from pasture on their own in the evening. Little did the boys know that one day they would make ordinary people

Steinau, as painted by younger brother Ludwig

This fishing scene is one of young Wilhelm's numerous paintings.
Jacob painted this picture of Steinau when he was ten years old.

like these famous with the stories they collected about goose girls and woodsmen, tailors and millers.

Holidays were always lively. Several times a year, the village square was filled with the sound of music and the beat of drums and with people exploring the stalls of a fair. At Eastertime the boys hunted for eggs that had been hidden on the green, and at Christmastime they'd look for apples that had been painted silver or gold and hidden by adults. If it snowed, they loved pelting the doors with snowballs, even if it did bring them scoldings from their father.

Town wasn't the only place where the brothers played. Some days after finishing chores like grinding coffee or gathering eggs for their mother, Jacob and Wilhelm headed out to the fields beyond the walls of the city. There they collected insects and feathers, stones, plants, and toads. Sometimes they drew their discoveries in their sketchbooks; other times they took things home to add to their collections or to trade with friends. Toads that didn't survive were buried in a swampy part of the garden.

In the fall they played war games with acorns, pretending that the single ones were foot soldiers, the double acorns officers, and the oddly shaped ones trumpeters or drummers. Sometimes the war would shift to the old city wall. There the unused guardhouses made great forts for the brothers, who used sticks to catapult apples at their imaginary enemies.

But Jacob and Wilhelm discovered that war was more than a game. At about the same time that the Grimms moved to Steinau a revolutionary war was breaking out in France, which lay next to Hesse. There, inspired in part by Thomas Jefferson's Declaration of Independence, which said that "all men are created equal," ordi-

Grandfather Zimmer

nary people were fighting against the government of the king. In January 1793, a mob beheaded King Louis XVI.

Jacob, who had been reading about the revolution in the newspaper, was shocked that people would kill a king, and he wrote a letter to his grandfather Zimmer, who still lived in Hanau. His grandfather's answer reveals a family attitude toward trouble that would become important for Jacob and Wilhelm later in their lives:

> *What you write, dear Jacob, about the murdered King in France and the unhappy prince he leaves behind, gives me welcome proof of your tender heart. We must remember that God, the supreme ruler, often permits evil so that His divine purpose may be fulfilled.*

Later, when difficult things happened to them, the Grimms would not complain but would try to look for something good that they believed God might be giving them in the midst of their trouble.

In the 1790s, trouble in France meant trouble in the German kingdoms as well. While Germany is one country today, it was made up of many different countries then, loosely organized as the Holy Roman Empire, and each of those countries had a king or a

HOLY ROMAN EMPIRE

From around 800 up until 1806 the kingdoms of central Europe were banded together in an alliance known as the Holy Roman Empire. There wasn't a country called Germany, but there were Germanic people in many of the countries that made up the empire. Throughout the years that Jacob and Wilhelm Grimm were growing up, Hesse, like many of the surrounding countries, was ruled by a noble called a *landgraf* (the closest English term is count).

A group of seven *landgraves* representing seven different kingdoms elected the emperor; such rulers were called electors, a title even more honorable than *landgraf*. While the emperor was supposed to help keep order in the empire, the electors usually chose a figurehead who would do little to lead the empire but much to make their particular families richer and stronger. In fact, the various kingdoms within the empire fought many wars among themselves about territory and religion, and the Holy Roman Empire grew weaker and weaker until Francis II, the last emperor, dissolved it when Napoleon conquered much of the region.

prince. That is one reason we meet so many kings and queens in the fairy tales: the stories came out of a land where entire kingdoms were about the size of a single state in the United States. But whatever the size of their kingdoms, large or small, none of these kings and princes liked what the revolutionaries in France were saying. These nobles didn't want to be overthrown or have their heads cut off.

And so when Jacob was ten and Wilhelm nine, the boys had sights more exciting than woodsmen and goose girls to watch. Countries surrounding France had been drawn into the war, and soldiers were wandering the streets of Steinau. Some wore the familiar uniform of their homeland and were relatively peaceful as they passed through. But the foreign troops were not so peaceful. Jacob and Wilhelm learned to stay clear of the Dutch soldiers, in their distinctive white uniforms, and to watch out for the black and yellow feathers on the helmets of the Austrian infantrymen. These soldiers, many of them retreating from the French, were often drunk and would use their swords to spear bread from the baker's and meat from the butcher's.

Dorothea Grimm forbade the boys to go outside when soldiers were passing through. But they would watch from the window, both thrilled and scared by the bizarre parades. The town and the countryside suffered from the looting. Slabs of bacon, strings of sausages, and slaughtered chickens hung from the soldiers' knapsacks. Mounted soldiers bored holes in loaves of bread and tied them to their horses. They were followed by whole wagonloads of dead oxen, pigs, and calves. Sometimes a prisoner, hands bound with chains or rope, staggered along in the ranks; sometimes the soldiers carried tame squirrels or ravens on their shoulders. There was a lot for two young boys to wonder about. Before going to bed, Jacob and Wilhelm often stared out their window at the campfires in the distance and wondered what adventures the soldiers were talking about as they sat there.

The disorderly soldiers made a lot of work for the magistrate, who had to investigate complaints about brandy drinkers who didn't pay their bills at the inn and soldiers who got into fights with townspeople. Philipp Grimm wasn't home much when soldiers were passing through Steinau.

But even if they didn't see him at dinnertime or in the evenings, Jacob and Wilhelm were proud of their father, with his pigtail and his uniform. Herr Grimm wore a blue frock coat with gold epaulettes and a red velvet collar over leather pants tucked into tall boots with silver spurs. It was an important-looking uniform, and the brothers knew that he was doing important work. Whenever his efforts to keep the peace didn't take him out of Steinau, Herr Grimm would read prayers with the family in the morning and ask them questions over dinner in the evening. Jacob and Wilhelm respected him and were eager to please him. There was a switch for punishment hanging behind the kitchen door, but years later Jacob couldn't remember that it was ever used. The brothers must have learned a lot about integrity and responsibility from watching their father do his work.

During quieter times, the boys hovered about the edges of the warm dining room of the Amtshaus when villagers and neighbors stopped by to visit their father. Innkeepers brought the registration forms of strangers for Herr Grimm's approval, and the men would sit at the large table smoking their pipes, drinking beer, and catching up on the day's news. If the boys were lucky, a woodsman might bounce them on his knee or another visitor, before leaving, hoist them into the driver's seat of his wagon so they could pretend to drive.

But pretending to be grown-up soon gave way to the need to act grown-up. During the Christmas holidays of 1795, Philipp Grimm became very sick with pneumonia. It must have been a difficult time for their mother; the previous April, the youngest Grimm, eight-month-old Georg, had died. And so it was perhaps to help his mother that Jacob kept Grandfather Zimmer posted on their father's health.

On January 5, 1796, the day after his eleventh birthday, Jacob wrote, explaining that their father was very weak and hadn't eaten for eight days. His weakness couldn't have been helped by the doctors' treatments. Like all good doctors of the period, they "bled" him five times, slicing a vein and collecting blood in a bowl in the belief that the illness was caused by an imbalance in the patient's body, an imbalance that could be corrected only if some of his blood was removed.

Jacob, however, was encouraged that his father seemed hungry and had asked for some bread from his favorite bakery in their old hometown: "Our dear father is regaining his appetite and would like some of baker Schüko's special bread. Mother asks if you would be so good as to send a small loaf. It must be freshly baked, since Father cannot eat anything dry." On January 8, Grandfather Zimmer sent the bread and wrote that he was happy at the sign of his son-in-law's improved health. But on January 10, 1796, Philipp Grimm died.

As the oldest son, Jacob now became the "man" of the family. He was the one who wrote the date of his father's death in the family Bible, where the Grimms, like most families of the time, kept a record of the important dates in their family's history.

Herr Grimm's death brought other changes as well. The family was forced to leave the official residence of the Amtmann. Since Dorothea Grimm had no job and they had little income, they discovered what it was like to be poor. They had to move twice in two years, first to a smaller rented house and then to a house that Dorothea managed to buy with the small pension that she received from the government because of her husband's former job. They were also helped by gifts from an aunt, Henrietta Zimmer, who was a lady-in-waiting to Countess Wilhelmine Karoline in nearby Kassel.

Everyone in the family had to work hard, and Jacob, in particular, felt the weight of family responsibilities. Once when someone in the village said bad things about Philipp Grimm, Jacob wrote to his grandfather to ask if the family could sue the person. It's clear that he thought of himself as the head of the family. And, indeed, a letter that he wrote to his aunt Zimmer in 1796 after another aunt had died shows how little this eleven-year-old sounded like a child:

> Dear and respected Aunt,
>
> I expect you have already heard from my grandfather of the death of my dear aunt. It is a bitter loss to us, but we thank God that He has put an end to her sufferings.
>
> You have, most esteemed Aunt, the sum of 400 talers on loan at 4% to Peter Mankel of Wachenbuchen. This man has paid no interest for three years. I have therefore called in the loan, for this state of affairs should not be allowed to

continue. If you wish, I will ask my mother to place it elsewhere. Or shall I send it to you in Kassel? We give thanks to God that my mother is well. She would have written to you herself but she is busy with the pig-slaughtering. She will write to you soon and send you some fresh sausage. I take the liberty of sending you a New Year greeting I have written myself, also one from my brother Wilhelm.

My brothers send their respects. Ferdinand was very ill but is better now. I have the honor to sign myself in all duty,

Your obedient nephew,
Jacob Grimm

While the brothers were not abandoned in the forest like Hansel and Gretel, the death of their father did leave them to face the world in a way that would change them forever. Their childhood was over.

CHAPTER TWO

School Days

Once upon a time there was an old goat who had seven young kids, and she loved them as much as any mother loves her children. One day she decided to go into the forest to fetch some food. So she called all seven of them to her and said, "Dear children, I want you to be on your guard against the wolf. If he gets in here, he'll eat you all up, skin and bones. That villain often disguises himself, but you can recognize him right away by his gruff voice and black feet."

—THE WOLF AND THE SEVEN YOUNG KIDS

We might have read a different story of "The Wolf and the Seven Young Kids" and "Hansel and Gretel" and the rest of the tales if Jacob and Wilhelm's aunt Henrietta had not arranged for them to attend a special school in Kassel. Their mother simply would not have been able to pay for them to go, and without the education the school gave them, they would probably have developed in another direction. Going to school wasn't easy for them, however. It meant moving away from their family and living on their own in a new city.

The trip to Kassel in September 1798 was an adventure, but it was also intimidating for twelve-year-old Wilhelm and thirteen-year-old Jacob. As they left Steinau for Hanau on the first stage of the journey, Wilhelm sat up in the front of the hired coach and cried as they passed all the familiar sights on the road to their old hometown. He felt as if there were a great canyon between their old life and the unknown life before them.

But if the journey was sometimes tearful, it was also exciting. At Hanau the brothers boarded a cargo boat on the Main River for the short sail to Frankfurt, where Grandfather Zimmer had arranged for them to spend the night under the care of his friend who was the head postmaster there. It also helped that Grandfather sent old Johann, his servant, to accompany the boys to the big city.

Compared with the villages where they had grown up, Frankfurt was enormous. When a boat docked at the wharf, a watchman blew a horn to announce the vessel's arrival, and the passengers would quickly be surrounded by the bustle and noise of the city. Fascinated by the crowds and the buildings, Jacob and Wilhelm walked the cobblestone streets past the cathedral where the emperor had been crowned. They didn't mind that Herr Rüppel, the postmaster, wasn't home. They just sat patiently on the steps and watched the bustling city until their grandfather's friend arrived and invited them in for lunch and coffee.

Before taking them to an inn, where they would spend the night before boarding a coach for the last stage of their journey to Kassel, Herr Rüppel treated the boys to an outing that made them forget their homesickness, at least for a while. They went to a wax museum, where they saw some fifty statues of famous people—emperors, kings, generals, a Who's Who of their part of the world. But best of all was the small circus, where they got to see animals they had only read about before—elephants, tigers, parrots, monkeys! Jacob was so excited that he wrote his mother all about it in a letter. Remembering how little money the family had, he added that while "it cost money," Herr Rüppel "paid for us too."

The next morning brought a ninety-mile coach ride into a new world. Their house in Steinau—and even Steinau's castle—was tiny compared to Schloss Wilhelmshöhe, the palace where Tante Zimmer served as lady-in-waiting to the countess, Wilhelmine Karoline, whose husband, Count Wilhelm I, ruled that region. Jacob and Wilhelm could hardly believe their eyes as the coach rolled through Kassel on the three-mile-long avenue that led straight through the city up to the hill on which the palace sat.

It seemed as if half of Steinau could fit inside Wilhelmshöhe.

Tante Henrietta Zimmer

The gardens of Wilhelmshöhe with the "guesthouse," Castle Lowenburg, on the left and the monument of Hercules on the top of the hill to the right

From the circular drive in front of the palace they could look with amazement at the statue of Hercules on the hilltop behind them. An earlier ruler of Hesse, Count Karl, had built it and the mile-long park filled with waterfalls and grottos in order to remind the people how powerful he was. The present ruler, Count Wilhelm, was even building another castle in the woods halfway up the hill-side as a guesthouse as well as a place where he could meet secretly with his mistresses. The turrets of the fake medieval castle were supposed to improve the view from Wilhelmshöhe. Ruins were the latest fad in landscape gardening.

Jacob and Wilhelm's quarters were not quite so fancy. They shared a room in the house of the third palace cook, Abraham

Vollbrecht, whose wife, their aunt assured their mother, kept a very orderly household. At a small writing desk beside the bed that they shared, they both worked on their lessons and on many letters home. There was much to write home about. But there were other things that they didn't want to tell their mother. Certainly, Kassel was exciting, but school—and their classmates—were sometimes less than exciting.

It wasn't that they didn't like to learn; in fact, Jacob and Wilhelm studied new things all their lives. The school that Tante Zimmer had enrolled them in—the Lyceum Fridericianum—was indeed a good school, but many of the students were connected to noble families or were pages who worked in the palace. Jacob and Wilhelm felt like country bumpkins. The teachers spoke to them differently from the way they spoke to the other students. German has two ways of saying *you*—one that is formal and respectful and another that is informal and condescending when used outside the family. The teachers talked respectfully to the students from Kassel but condescendingly to Jacob and Wilhelm.

Making matters worse was the discovery that the brothers were far behind the other students their age. Apparently, Herr Zinckhan's lessons hadn't helped them much. Jacob was perhaps right when he said that he had learned little from the old school-master except how to pay attention to a teacher. The school tested new students before placing them in a class, and Jacob just managed to make it into the lowest of the university preparatory classes. Wilhelm didn't qualify and had to study with a private tutor for a year before he could be admitted.

The school comprised seven classes, or grades. The top four grades prepared students for study at a university, while the lowest three were designed for students who didn't plan to go on with school or work at a special profession. Since each grade normally took two years to complete, Jacob, now thirteen, would have been twenty-one years old before he graduated from the lyceum.

Fortunately for both brothers, however, they were able to move through the grades more quickly than most students. But such advancement came at a price—a lot of hard studying and very little time for leisure. Each day they spent six hours at school, studying such subjects as geography, natural history, anthropology, natural philosophy (what is now called physics), logic, and moral philosophy. And before they went to school, they spent four or five hours daily being tutored in Latin and French by the Court Master of Pages, Dietmar Stöhr, an eccentric old man who would shave and have the wigmaker powder his hair during their lessons. But he was a teacher whom they liked much better than their other instructors.

This difficult routine made the brothers grow even closer. It didn't help that their family expected a lot from them. Soon after they arrived, Grandfather Zimmer reminded them that school wasn't something to be taken lightly:

> *I cannot repeat often enough that you must remember your goal, the reason for being where you are. This means diligence during lessons and away from them, so that you may lay the foundations for your future good, do yourselves credit, and give joy to your mother, to me and to the whole family. Therefore, stay away from company which might lead you into temptation, but associate with sensible people*

from whom you can profit, and, above all, fear the Lord,
which is the beginning of all wisdom. It will give your old
grandfather great joy at all times to have good news from you.

Even as Grandfather Zimmer urged the boys to take life seriously, he reminded their aunt that the boys had large appetites.

Tante Zimmer, of course, did see to it that the boys got enough to eat. Yet Jacob and Wilhelm may have been getting discouraged. Wilhelm wrote to his mother, saying how much he missed her but asking her not to tell their aunt about his homesickness because he knew how much it cost Tante Zimmer to send them to school in Kassel. Thus, a week or two after they had received the warning from their grandfather, their mother wrote to Wilhelm, giving a similar warning and advising him to stay focused on his schoolwork:

> *I remind you, my son, to be diligent, particularly at home.*
> *You must do without many pleasures just now. Do not look*
> *around for company of other boys, or you will become too*
> *distracted and also be a nuisance to your good landlord.*
> *Wilhelm, do use this heaven-sent opportunity, and remember*
> *that if it pleased the Lord to call me or your good aunt,*
> *everything would be finished immediately, and you would be*
> *forced to do something else. Also, remember how you and*
> *your brother have advantages, not granted to your brothers*
> *and sister on whom the same amount of money cannot be*
> *spent. You must not compare yourself to other young people*
> *of your age who may go out and enjoy themselves. Perhaps*

they still have both their parents. But you no longer have a father, and that matters a lot. Jacob can help you with anything you do not know in your studies, as you are still much behind him. God keep you both in health, and may He bless your work.

Perhaps it's not surprising that Dorothea Grimm wanted to remind the boys of death and its consequences. Their Tante Schlemmer had died the same year as their father and, in the twelve years before that, their mother had watched three of her children die. She wanted the boys to be prepared in case any of the other adults in their lives died. Life was fragile. Yes, God protected them, but sometimes, for reasons that they couldn't understand, He let things happen to his people.

If the family's expectations weighed heavily on the brothers, they didn't complain. In fact, even away from home and in the midst of all their schoolwork, they felt a kind of responsibility for their younger brothers and sister. Wilhelm's letters to seven-year-old Charlotte, whom the family called Lotte, sound a lot like the letters Grandfather Zimmer wrote to him in Kassel—loving, but full of advice on how to be good:

> *To my dear little sister Malchen,*
>
> *I have found a pretty little sheet of paper in my chest, and I thought to myself, you must congratulate dear Malchen on being very good, knitting diligently, being obedient to Mother, and keeping me in her heart.*
>
> *Dear Malchen, will you not soon learn to write letters? Once you are able, you must write to our good aunt, and*

thank her for the beautiful fur coat. Do write to me, too, and
I will send you some little notes which you can put into your
knitting bag.

Both Wilhelm and Jacob were constantly aware of how much they and their siblings benefited from the generosity of their aunt Zimmer. Clearly, they had taken note of the lesson that their mother had wanted them to learn.

Holidays must have been lonely for the brothers. They didn't even get to go home during their Christmas vacation. Instead, they would spend Christmas with their aunt and some of her acquaintances in Kassel, writing letters to their family instead of celebrating with them. There was a hint of sadness behind the greetings that they wrote. They would ask about their sister and brothers and tell their mother how much they loved her and then would explain what they did on the holiday.

Tante Zimmer saw to it that the boys received presents. On their second Christmas in Kassel, Jacob told his mother that their aunt had given them each the same presents: a little calendar, a good-looking nightcap, some apple and pear candy, an apple stuck with coins, and some material for new vests.

Yet not all of their time in Kassel was taken up with thinking of their family and other serious matters. Even with attending classes and being tutored, writing letters and copying notes, Jacob and Wilhelm found a little time for fun. They made a couple of good friends—Paul Wigand, the son of a university professor, and Baron Ernst von der Malsburg, the son of a colonel whose family was well connected in court circles. The boys explored Kassel together, Jacob sometimes shouting, "I've discovered another new

Siblings

Jacob and Wilhelm had three brothers who died before they were one year old. Friedrich Hermann Georg was born in December 1783 and died in March 1784. Friedrich was born in June 1791 and died in August 1791. Georg Eduard was born in July 1794 and died in April 1795.

Of their four living siblings, Jacob and Wilhelm were closest to Ludwig (1790–1863), whom they called Louis, and Charlotte (1793–1833), whom they called Lotte or Malchen. Ludwig grew up to be a well-known artist and illustrated an edition of *Household Tales* as well as painted numerous scenes of places where the brothers had lived. Charlotte married Ludwig Hassenpflug, a member of the family that furnished many folktales for the brothers' collection. Carl (1787–1852) fought as a soldier against Napoleon but after the war had little idea of what to do with his life. He finally went into business and eventually wrote a book himself—on accounting! Ferdinand (1788–1845) worried Jacob and Wilhelm more than any of their other siblings. He did not seem to be disciplined or to take life seriously enough in their view. Although Ferdinand worked off and on in a Berlin publishing house for almost twenty years, he was financially supported by his older brothers during the last ten years of his life.

street!" as they made their way into un-familiar neighborhoods. And on one of their excursions into the countryside, they may even have passed by the cottage of Frau Dorothea Viehmann, the

Fairy Tale Wife, who a few years later would tell them many stories for their collection of fairy tales.

On Sundays when it was warm or on days when they had a half holiday from school, they would head for the parks around the palace. It's more than likely that some of the white-wigged gentlemen and long-gowned ladies enjoying the promenade at Wilhelmshöhe shook their heads—and maybe their canes!—at the boys running with nets on long poles to catch butterflies. Collecting butterflies, leaves, stones—all sorts of natural objects—gave some relief from their studies. In fact, late in his life Jacob said that if he had to choose his career over again, he would choose botany, so great was his love of plants and nature.

When there was less time to get away, Paul and Jacob and Wilhelm haunted the secondhand shops for books and pictures. If they had a little extra pocket money—which was not often—they would buy books of poetry or fiction for their personal libraries. They loved to read, and they devoured books without thinking about what was good or bad literature. Over their years at the lyceum, however, their tastes grew more toward poetry and ballads. When bored in class, Paul and Jacob would pass notes back and forth, writing silly nonsense poems together.

In the evenings or if there wasn't enough time to get away for even a brief outing, Jacob and Wilhelm would pick up their sketchbooks. Sometimes they drew the Grimm coat of arms or scenes from Steinau. At other times they sketched objects in their room or from around Kassel. Although they never reached the level of their younger brother Ludwig Emil, who became a famous artist in Germany, they did, at least by their own admission, draw pretty well. Thinking back on their drawing during this time, Jacob said that "we made considerable progress without any teaching."

The brothers made considerable progress in their schoolwork as well. After Jacob's first year of study the teachers overcame their prejudice against him and commended him "as one of the ablest, most diligent and well-behaved pupils." Wilhelm received similar praise after he entered the university preparatory program, but he remained almost a year behind Jacob in his studies.

By the spring of 1802 Jacob was ready to go to the university. The lyceum didn't give exams or hold graduation ceremonies.

Jacob painted the coat of arms of the Grimm family. The motto reads, "Honesty is the best policy in life."

Students could simply ask to go to the university when they were ready.

But it wasn't so simple in Jacob's case. German society was divided into many categories or levels, and because of overcrowding at the universities, the Hessian rulers had decreed that only the top seven levels of society could attend a university. The son of a magistrate fell into the eighth level and was thus prohibited from attending.

There was, however, a way to request special permission, and Dorothea Grimm wrote to Count Wilhelm requesting an exception to the rule. On April 6, 1802, the Grimms received the good news. Jacob had been accepted at the university in Marburg, a city thirty or so miles from Kassel.

But the good news for Jacob's career was hard news for the brothers' friendship. For the first time in their lives Jacob and Wilhelm would be living apart.

CHAPTER THREE

Into the World

Then the old man accompanied them part of the way, and when they were about to take their leave, he gave them a shiny knife and said, "If ever you should separate, stick this knife into a tree at the crossroad. Then if one of you comes back, he can see how his absent brother is doing, for the side of the blade facing the direction that he took will rust if he's dying but will stay bright as long as he's alive."

—THE TWO BROTHERS

Marburg was something of a shock to Jacob after Steinau and Kassel. There had been a slight hill leading up the street from the Amtshaus to the town square, and Wilhelmshöhe had rested on a hill above Kassel. But he hadn't imagined that a city could be built right on a steep hillside as this university town was.

The only way to get to the university was by walking up the cobblestone streets that zigzagged back and forth up the hillside. The angles were so steep that the walk from the river at the edge of town to the university was like a mountain hike. Stone stairs provided shortcuts through some of the switchbacks. It seemed to Jacob that there were steps everywhere.

At the top of the hill sat the castle that guarded the city. Several hundred steps and one or two switchbacks below it, the buildings of the university clung to the hillside. About midway in the climb to the castle and perhaps a quarter of a mile below the university, a sharp turn in the streets led into the town square, where all sorts of things were sold on market days. Conveniently, Jacob found a house just about a block above that, so the walk to classes was not severe. Still, as he wrote to his friend Paul, he was amazed that one could walk into a house from the street and be on its top floor.

In some ways life at the university was not too different from life at the school in Kassel. First of all, there were only two hundred or so students. Although it was the oldest Protestant university in Europe, it wasn't as large as the universities in Heidelberg or Berlin. And if the university's size reminded Jacob of the lyceum, the teachers did as well. He didn't like them.

Even as a first-year student he was critical of his classes, which bored him. Most of the professors read their lectures and expected the students, sitting on hard wooden benches and leaning forward to write on a slanted board that served as a desk for the entire row of students, to copy them down word for word. He wrote his friend that he filled almost two sheets of paper per hour, joking that a dog couldn't sneeze without his having to copy it down. (Once Jacob even got scolded for reading a letter that he had just received.) But in his letters Jacob's judgments were harsh. Too many professors emphasized facts that would be on their tests instead of ideas that would make students think. And while Professor Wachler's lectures were satisfactory, his teaching was superficial. Professor Erxleben's lectures were monotonous and old-fashioned. Jacob could tolerate Professor Weiss's lectures on Greek and Roman law. At least *he* was a lively speaker and seemed to know his subject. Nonetheless, he occasionally said things that Jacob thought were too casual and, therefore, inappropriate.

Jacob's seriousness about his studies earned him the nickname "the old man" from his fellow students. Part of the problem was that Jacob had read more books and was brighter than most of the other students. Also the subject he was studying—law—did not really interest him. For family reasons Jacob had chosen to study it, but he was more interested in history, literature, and even botany. His mother had hoped that he would work at the same profession as his father had, and his father himself had often discussed legal matters with him and Wilhelm, indicating a desire that the boys follow his path. Law was not only a practical subject to study, it offered a way of pleasing a mother who had sacrificed much for his schooling.

The strangeness of Marburg and his dislike of his studies added to the loneliness Jacob felt on account of his separation from Wilhelm. His one relief from the routine was to take walks in the surrounding countryside, which he found "with each step more romantic and beautiful." He would walk in the meadows or sit beneath a tree and watch Marburg's castle at the top of the mountain glowing golden in the evening sun. But in the midst of his walks his sense of loneliness would return, and he wrote to Paul that he would rather be in a wooden stall in a barn with friends than all alone in this beautiful scene.

Since Paul knew how lonely Jacob was, he might have worried briefly when Jacob wrote that he hoped to receive one more letter from Paul after which they would never see each other again in this world. Fortunately, Jacob went on to explain that a certain group of people believed that God was going to destroy the world on September 13, 1802, because it was so godless and wicked. Obviously the world didn't end, and Jacob dug into his studies to forget about his loneliness.

The brothers' separation was made all the more difficult by the fact that Wilhelm had a severe asthma attack during the fall of 1802, when Jacob moved to Marburg. Of course, while his brother's illness must have added to Jacob's loneliness, Wilhelm's sense of isolation had to have been even greater. Wilhelm had earlier been ill with scarlet fever, from which he had recovered, although increasingly he had trouble breathing. Looking back on this time, he wrote: "I began to suffer from shortness of breath, soon accompanied by pains in the chest. The way to the lyceum was frequently bitter as I struggled against the cold wind that blows so often across the Friedrichsplatz [a large square in the middle of Kassel]."

As he recovered, Wilhelm was confined to his room for six months. The only activity that he was allowed was to sketch and draw. He was not even supposed to read or write! Fortunately, Paul Wigand would stop by every day to tell him about school and to help him write letters to Jacob. Wilhelm later claimed that he learned from being sick. He used the hours at night when he couldn't sleep or during the day when he couldn't work to think about who he was and what he wanted to do with his life.

Perhaps those hours of thoughtfulness helped him work all the harder when he finally returned to school, because even with so much time away from the classroom, he managed to advance in his studies. By June 1803 the school's new principal, Herr Cäsar, one of those teachers who had spoken so condescendingly to the brothers when they arrived at the lyceum, had only glowing things to say about Wilhelm. In his report, he said that Wilhelm was "endowed by nature with outstanding talents." He had made "excellent progress" in his four years at the school. Moreover, "during this period his diligence and blameless behavior were an example to his fellow pupils." In fact, the principal added, Wilhelm "could be numbered among the foremost men of letters." We could almost regard his words as prophetic if he hadn't added the self-serving phrase "if he continued his studies at the lyceum."

Nathaniel Cäsar, teacher and later rector of the lyceum in Kassel, drawn by Ludwig

Once more Dorothea Grimm wrote to Count Wilhelm, this time requesting permission for Wilhelm to go to the university at Marburg. Permission was granted, and the brothers were reunited. Unlike the coach trip from Steinau to Kassel, this trip to a new home gave Wilhelm no reason to shed tears; after a year apart he would be living with Jacob again. Instead of exchanging letters every month, they could talk the way they used to, discussing their teachers after a lecture, sorting through the day's events before falling asleep at night, wondering together what

Lotte or Ludwig, Carl or Ferdinand might be up to. Once more Jacob and Wilhelm were sharing a room and studying together.

Jacob had much to show Wilhelm. There were Marburg's zigzagging streets to explore and steps to climb. There were new books to talk about and new bookstores to browse in. Now they could walk the meadows and the hills around Marburg together. Now Jacob wouldn't be alone on his trips to watch the sun set behind Marburg's hilltop castle. Now the brothers could marvel together at the grandeur of Marburg's Church of Saint Elisabeth. Saint Elisabeth, who had lived in the thirteenth century, was famous for giving to the poor, caring for the sick, and performing miracles. But what must have caught Jacob and Wilhelm's attention as they visited the church was her glass coffin in a large alcove near the front of the sanctuary. Residents of Marburg still like to claim that it was this coffin that inspired the brothers to include the glass coffin in their version of "Snow White," even though it seems as though the coffin was in the story when they first recorded it.

The university demanded hard work and long hours, but Jacob and Wilhelm found time for friends as well. Paul Wigand joined them at the university, though he almost didn't get in because he wasn't from an upper-class family. When he first showed up for class, the professor asked to see the letter of permission from the count. Without it or some other connection to the court, he would have been sent away. Fortunately, Paul's father had been given a small job by the count, and Paul was able to mention that and get into the class. Nonetheless, he and Jacob and Wilhelm were reminded once again of the class differences in their society.

Another old companion from Kassel, Ernst von der Malsburg, didn't have any problem getting into the university. He came from a noble family, one of the richest in the region. Ernst introduced the brothers to several wealthy families in Marburg, so even though they didn't have much pocket money, they had upper-class entertainment. While many of their fellow students were gambling, drinking great quantities of beer, and even fighting duels, the Grimms met with friends in less rowdy parties. In the evenings, they would discuss books, dance, or even act out plays like Shakespeare's *Midsummer Night's Dream*. Although they were always aware of class differences, Jacob and Wilhelm's earlier training in dancing and their experiences in Kassel helped them fit into upper-class society. They dressed the part, wearing high-collared white shirts beneath scarlet frock coats with black velvet collars, and tight tan leather pants tucked into tall black boots. Imitating the other students, they even wore spurs on their boots.

Like his brother, Wilhelm chose to study law, but he had the advantage of having his brother's advice on which professors to choose. As time went on, Jacob had come to respect more of his professors, particularly Friedrich Karl von Savigny, a fairly young teacher whose family owned land between Hanau and Steinau, the two towns where Jacob and Wilhelm had lived as boys. Both brothers liked the way that Savigny taught. Whereas many other professors dictated lectures that they expected students to copy down and memorize, Savigny lectured as though he was talking to the students, sometimes quoting poetry to illustrate a point and frequently pausing to ask them questions. Like a modern teacher, he sometimes would assign papers for them to write that he would, in turn, write comments on. As ordinary as that sounds today, it was extraordinary in 1803.

Professor von Savigny recognized Jacob and Wilhelm's gifts and love of learning, and his relationship with the brothers soon moved beyond the classroom. Because they loved to read and discuss books, he invited them over to his house, where their lives took on a new direction. Years later Jacob still remembered walking into Savigny's library and running his eyes over the books that

Professor Friedrich Karl von Savigny

entirely covered the walls. What a grand experience for an avid book lover! In one of those visits a volume of German songs from the Middle Ages caught his eye. Jacob said that when he picked it up and read the lyrics "in a strange German that I only half understood," a "strange feeling" came over him. He didn't know then that he was starting down the path to collecting fairy tales and studying the German language, or that he would read that book more than twenty times from cover to cover. He didn't even feel brave enough to borrow it from his professor.

Savigny taught the Grimms how to be careful researchers and thoughtful scholars, lessons that would be useful later when they collected folktales. He also pointed them toward the literary heritage of their own country, impressing on them that German history and ideas were as important as the Greek and Roman ideas that were emphasized in lectures at Marburg and most other universities. A new generation of writers and artists, who called their art Romantic, were looking to common people and to nature for ideas. Instead of writing about the lives of nobles, they wrote about simple shepherds or shoemakers, and they loved the traditional songs and stories of ordinary people. Savigny not only introduced Jacob and Wilhelm to these ideas, he also introduced them to some actual writers, some of whom remained lifelong friends of the Grimms.

On evening visits to their professor's house Jacob and Wilhelm would sip tea flavored with red wine and listen to people like the poet Clemens Brentano and the writer Achim von Arnim. Brentano was a flamboyant, moody person whose father had wanted him to go into business but whose habits of wearing bright orange and green clothes and of breaking appointments got him out of the business world. On these evenings with the Grimms, Brentano and Arnim would talk excitedly about the folk songs that they were collecting for a book that would become famous in Germany — *The Boy's Magic Horn.*

Later, when Jacob and Wilhelm's books were *more* famous, Brentano would brag that he had started the brothers down the path toward fame. Actually, he had almost prevented their fame by borrowing — and then losing — the manuscript of their folktales just before it was to be published. It is fortunate that Jacob and Wilhelm had copied it before lending it to Brentano. We can say that it is fortunate, too, that the brothers met these entertaining writers and turned their own thoughts toward German literature instead of the law.

Wilhelm had been at the university a year when Professor von Savigny left Marburg for Paris to conduct research at the Bibliothèque Nationale, the French national library, for a book on Roman law. Jacob and Wilhelm felt the loss of their favorite professor, but they had no idea how soon they would hear from him or what enormous impact he would have on their lives. In late 1804 the brothers received intriguing news from their friend Ernst von der Malsburg, who had been in Paris visiting his uncle, the Hessian ambassador to France, that Professor von Savigny had lost a trunk containing notes for his book and that his eyes were bothering him too much to continue the research by himself. He wanted to hire a research assistant, and Jacob was one of the two students whom he was considering for the job.

An invitation came to Jacob soon afterward. Accepting it would mean dropping out of school and delaying the time when he could get his degree in law and a job that could support the family.

It would mean turning aside from his parents' dream for his life. It would also mean moving away from Wilhelm again.

Jacob wrote letters to his mother and to Tante Zimmer asking for their permission to go to Paris, and both women said yes. What Jacob didn't know was that his mother was sick when she received his letter—so sick, it seems, that the doctor almost didn't tell her about the letter from her son. History might have been very different if he hadn't shown it to her or if she had insisted that Jacob stay at the university and become a lawyer. But she didn't. In fact, in her reply she didn't even let Jacob know that she was sick. Later, Jacob found out from his sister, Lotte, that each night their mother rose from her sickbed and stood staring out the window, as if wishing she could see all the way to Paris to discover how Jacob was doing during the cold winter in a strange country.

It's probably a good thing that Jacob didn't know about his mother's illness or her worries, and it's probably good that he didn't realize how difficult the separation from Wilhelm would be, because he did accept Savigny's offer to work in the national library. That experience, lonely as it was, did much to shape both brothers' lives.

The trip to Paris took ten days in a coach that also carried the mail. We don't know the reason, but Jacob kept track of the hours it took to travel from stop to stop—160 hours in all. He also kept track of his money, of which he had very little. Things in Paris seemed very expensive to him. Upon his arrival, he wrote to his mother that he had only two of his ten karolin coins left—a conductor had overcharged him, and he had been given a counterfeit coin in change. But life with his much-respected professor, Jacob assured her, was more than comfortable. He had a beautiful little room and they ate very well, sometimes even at a restaurant (which was the French word for *guest kitchen,* Jacob explained) that featured real silver service.

Jacob also dashed off a letter to Wilhelm. While he hadn't seen anything as beautiful as the countryside around Marburg, he admitted that the valleys of the Rhine River in Germany and the Marne River in France were also beautiful. The majestic cathedral in Metz, Jacob rattled on, was the most beautiful he had ever seen. There was nothing like it in Paris. Even Savigny agreed, Jacob said.

But while Jacob was writing excitedly about his trip, Wilhelm was writing Jacob a letter in a sadder mood. When he realized Jacob was really gone, Wilhelm wrote, he thought that his heart would break. It was so hard not having his brother there to talk with. In fact, sometimes when he was sitting alone by their library, he would hear the floorboards creak and be startled, thinking that Jacob was there as well. The letters that the brothers sent each other often traveled for two or three weeks before being delivered, and so it was some time before each knew what the other was feeling.

After the initial excitement of his trip wore off, Jacob, too, began to miss Wilhelm more intensely, worrying when he didn't hear from him. He urged Wilhelm to write him about everything that was happening, even gossip, because, he said, things that might seem "trivial or small at home" become "things to cherish" in a foreign country.

Jacob was clearly concerned about Wilhelm, recommending that his brother not work too hard at his studies, reminding him that he couldn't afford to get sick again. He also suggested that

Wilhelm invite Paul Wigand to move in with him, which Paul did for a short while. But Paul wasn't as quiet or studious as Wilhelm, and the two of them soon argued and split up. Eventually, Paul and Wilhelm got over their hard feelings and renewed their friendship, which lasted for the rest of their lives, but this experience and Jacob's trip to Paris strengthened the brothers' commitment

TALERS

Jacob and Wilhelm were paid in talers (also spelled thalers). While it is difficult to compute the value of nineteenth-century talers in twenty-first-century dollars, it *is* possible to get a sense of the taler's worth by comparing nineteenth-century rates and prices.

These varied from place to place, of course, but in 1798 one taler would buy eight pounds of beef or one pound of coffee. One taler would purchase a bottle of wine, a pound of cheese, and three loaves of bread. In 1800 persons traveling without a servant and sharing a carriage could expect to pay a bit more than one taler per mile for all their expenses (transportation, food, and lodging). In 1809 one taler would pay the postage to ship a woolen coat from Kassel to Berlin.

Less than two months' worth of medicine cost Wilhelm almost thirty talers during his stay in Halle in 1809. The yearly rent of the brothers' apartment in Berlin was 475 talers, at a time when they were each earning 1,000 talers annually plus additional income from the publication of books and articles.

Prices like these suggest something of how difficult it must have been for the whole family to live on Jacob's salary of 1,000 talers per year during to each other. In July 1805, when he was thinking about going back to Hesse, Jacob wrote to Wilhelm that "they must never be apart" and that "any separation could make him die from grief." Wilhelm answered that he felt the same, that "no one loved me as much as you and my love for you is just as heartfelt."

But before he could return to live with his brother, Jacob had

---

King Jérôme's reign, not to mention the 100 talers per year that he received at his first job. Tante Zimmer's financial help was crucial to their survival.

The history of the taler reflects the history of the region. The silver coins were first minted in 1519 in Joachimthal, when large amounts of silver were discovered in the area. First called Joachimthalers, the coins eventually became termed talers, and numerous versions of talers were issued until 1871, when they were replaced by the mark as the unit of currency.

Since any kingdom or independent city could mint its own talers, there were occasional complications in spending the coins in territories other than the one in which they were made. To attempt to solve this problem, the kingdoms hammered out an agreement in 1837: twelve pfennigs would equal one groschen, and thirty groschen would equal one taler.

By the time they were replaced in Germany, talers had been used widely in trading, and the term had spread around the world in a way that would have no doubt fascinated the brothers—becoming *daalers* in Holland, *dalers* in Denmark, and *dollars* in America.

to finish his work in Paris. Every day he went to the national library, where he sat from ten o'clock in the morning until two o'clock in the afternoon, reading old manuscripts. Many of the books had been written in the Middle Ages, before the printing press had been invented, and thus had been copied by hand by monks or scholars. Jacob's job was to compare different versions of the same books to discover which were the most accurate. The fact that Jacob found this exciting and not tiresome shows that already at the age of twenty he was on the way to his life's work. In fact, he used this opportunity to look up the original manuscript of the book of German songs that had caught his eye in Savigny's library in Marburg. Wilhelm's interest in old literature was growing too, and he repeatedly urged Jacob to look for old German manuscripts. In almost every letter they talked about books as well as about the things happening in their daily lives.

It was in October, ten months after he had left for Paris, that Jacob was finally reunited with Wilhelm in Marburg. The brothers spent several joy-filled days together before traveling to Kassel, where their mother had moved in order to be close to her sister and their aunt, Tante Zimmer. When they got to their family's new house, their mother was out visiting their aunt for the evening. So eager were they to meet her that they set out through the dark streets to find her. When they met her walking home carrying a lantern, they had a joyful reunion in the streets.

For the first time in seven years the whole family was living together again. The younger children went to school in Kassel, while Wilhelm looked for work and prepared for his final examinations at the university, which he hoped to take the following spring. Jacob decided not to take his final exams; they weren't absolutely necessary, particularly if a student had good recommendations, and Jacob felt certain that he did. He hoped to work as a lawyer or secretary for the government, positions that, like most significant jobs, were granted by the count. He had heard from Tante Zimmer that Count Wilhelm had seen one of the letters he had written for the Hessian ambassador from Paris and had been impressed with his talent.

Unfortunately, all the available positions had been snatched up by others, and so the Grimms had to live without any income for several months. Tante Zimmer, as always, assisted with the finances. It helped, too, that Dorothea Grimm had butchered a pig and made sausages before she moved from the country town to Kassel.

Finally, in January 1806 the count made Jacob a clerk in the Hessian war office. The work, copying letters and other papers, was dull after Jacob's exciting time in Paris, and it didn't help that he had to wear a stiff uniform and powdered pigtail. And while it gave the family some income, it didn't give much—one hundred talers, or about seventy dollars, a year. Then, too, the very fact that Hesse needed a war office was a sign of trouble. Napoleon and his armies were conquering Europe. Big changes were in store for the province of Hesse and for the Grimms.

CHAPTER FOUR

War

However, the other brother, who was standing near the golden lilies at home, saw one of the lilies suddenly droop. "Oh, God!" he said. "My brother's had a great accident. I've got to go and see if I can save him."

—THE GOLDEN CHILDREN

The brothers knew that Napoleon's invasion put danger all around them. When they had been much younger, taking lessons from Herr Zinckhan in Steinau, Napoleon Bonaparte had been taking control of the French army and gradually, bit by bit, conquering sections of Europe and the Mediterranean: first Italy, then Egypt and Syria, then Austria, the Netherlands, and the provinces of Germany. In December 1804, shortly before Jacob joined Savigny in Paris, Napoleon was dissolving the French republic and crowning himself emperor of all France's lands. In 1805, when Jacob was returning to Germany from Paris, he had to alter his route to avoid Napoleon's armies, and by 1806 the Holy Roman Empire had ended. That fall, after the leaves turned colors and the nights began to be colder, Wilhelm looked out his window and saw the campfires of French soldiers in the fields around Kassel. He could hardly believe that the country he loved was to be overrun by foreigners.

On the morning of November 1, 1806, French soldiers marched into Kassel, and French officials took over the government. The count fled to Denmark, and the countess fled to the nearby city of Gotha, to take refuge in the court of the prince of that area. Tante Zimmer went with her, but the Grimms stayed in Kassel. Napoleon combined the territory of Hesse with other nearby territories and called the unified region the Kingdom of Westphalia. He put his youngest brother, Jérôme Bonaparte, on the throne of Westphalia. The palace Wilhelmshöhe was renamed Napoleonshöhe. Foreigners filled Kassel; new customs rose up almost overnight; the sound of people talking German was replaced by the sound of people talking French. It seemed to Wilhelm that no other German city had undergone so many changes.

Now that Hesse no longer officially existed, the Hessian war office, where Jacob worked, was changed into a supply department for the French armies. Because of his excellent knowledge of French, Jacob was invited to continue working in the office. But for the same reason much of the tedious work fell on his shoulders, and he quickly tired of the job. Feeling that he didn't get any rest day or night, Jacob decided to quit the job *and* quit working with the law.

He had heard about a job in the royal library; with his training in the history of literature and his experience of working with handwritten manuscripts, he thought that he was a natural for the job. Indeed, he might have been the best qualified person, but he didn't get the job. Meanwhile, Wilhelm had passed his exams at the university, but he had no better luck than Jacob at finding work in Kassel. Both he and Jacob did bring in a little bit of money by writing literary articles, but by and large the family was once again without any income.

Tante Zimmer helped out as much as she could with money

NAPOLEON

Napoleon Bonaparte (1769–1821) was one of the most famous military leaders in history. When the French people overthrew their king in the 1790s, Napoleon became an officer in the revolutionary army. After he led his troops on successful campaigns in Italy and then over the Alps into Austria, where he forced the Austrians to surrender, Napoleon became a popular hero in France and throughout Europe. After additional successes in Egypt and Turkey, he returned to Paris, where he maneuvered his way to the title of emperor, becoming known as Napoleon I. As emperor, Napoleon reorganized the laws and expanded education and the arts in France. He also expanded France's territory, spreading its influence through Holland, Switzerland, Prussia, and the German nations, eventually attacking Great Britain and Russia. He had his eyes on the New World, but when his efforts in the Caribbean were halted, he sold the Louisiana Territory to the United States, thus doubling the size of the country. Eventually, the combined European powers, led by Great Britain, defeated Napoleon, forcing him to live out the rest of his life in exile on an island.

and even packages of food, but this was a dark and difficult time for the family. It became even darker and more difficult when, in May 1808, Dorothea Grimm became sick and died. Jacob said later that as her children stood around her deathbed, they didn't know how to comfort each other. He, in particular, felt that he had let her down by being unemployed. "Had she only lived a few months more," he said wistfully, "how truly happy she would have been at my improved position."

Those few months until Jacob received a position were not easy ones. The small pension that the family had received because of their father's work stopped when their mother died. Lotte ironed and mended clothes for the family and made cravats (a kind of necktie) for her brothers out of a white dress she had outgrown. They sent to Steinau for butter and other supplies, which were cheaper there than in Kassel. Neighbors also shared some foodstuffs with them. But even with these measures it was hard to make ends meet, so they cut back to eating one meal a day and stopped drinking tea in the evening because sugar was so expensive.

When circumstances were difficult, the brothers relied on their love for each other and their faith in God. "In all tribulations," Wilhelm wrote Tante Zimmer, "we will remain united in love." And even though his health was only "tolerable," he told Savigny, the thought of it didn't distress him, for "with a grateful heart," he saw "every day as a gift from God."

In July the brothers had more to be thankful for. A friend spoke to King Jérôme about Jacob, and the king put him in charge of the library at the palace. The library had about twelve thousand books, and the only people permitted to use them, other

Dorothea Grimm, in a portrait painted just after she died

than the librarian, were the king and queen, neither of whom, it turned out, was very interested in reading. Jacob's only specific instruction was to write the words "Library of the King" in large letters on the door. What he did with his time was up to him as long as he followed the many rules of the new French government. Paul Wigand had turned down the same job because he hated the French, but Jacob was more tolerant, especially, as he explained to Savigny, since it was "very urgent" for them to earn some money. Except for the French supervision, the position was ideal. Jacob could study whatever interested him *and* be paid for it.

Apparently, the king was pleased with whatever he thought Jacob was doing because he soon gave Jacob a raise in pay and put him on a special council that advised the king, the only

German in such a position. Jacob was now making ten times more money than he had been in his old job at the Hessian war office. But with added security also came some problems—and not just the fact that Jacob had to wear a fancy uniform when he attended the king's councils, a kind of showiness that he disliked. His position in the government made him a Westphalian citizen, and Westphalian citizens could be drafted into the army. Although he had played army with Wilhelm when he was younger, he didn't want to fight in a real army now, and certainly not in support of the French. Luckily, when it came his turn to draw a number in the lottery that was used to pick soldiers, he drew a safe number. He could stay with his books and with his brother.

Yet he didn't get to stay with Wilhelm very long. The culprit was sickness, not war. Wilhelm's health was getting steadily worse. Climbing even a few steps took his breath away, and he had fierce pains in his chest and an apparently serious problem with his heart. "The pain," Wilhelm said later, "which I could only compare to the sensation of a fiery arrow being shot through my heart from time to time, left me with a constant feeling of anxiety." Sometimes his heart would beat violently and then, just as suddenly, it would beat normally again. A number of times these strange heartbeats lasted as long as twenty hours, and Wilhelm would sit awake, wondering if he was going to die. Yet, once again, in the face of trouble, Wilhelm held on to a positive attitude:

> *Many a sleepless night, I sat upright, without moving, waiting for the dawn to give me some comfort. A quail, hanging in a cage by a neighbor's window, was often the first to announce the dawn, and even now I cannot hear that bird's*

strange call with indifference. It is incredible how much one can physically endure throughout the years, without losing the joy of life. The feeling of youth may have helped, but I was not completely depressed by my sickness, and went on working, even with pleasure, when things were tolerable. I didn't deceive myself about my condition, and I considered every day that I still lived as a gift from God.

Because he was so sick, Wilhelm decided to travel some sixty miles to the city of Halle to be treated by Professor Johann Reil, who was famous for his medical practice. While Professor Reil's treatments may have sounded promising in 1809 when Wilhelm visited him, they sound like torture today. When he got up in the mornings, Wilhelm rubbed his neck with a strong mercury oint-ment—which doctors today recognize as a poison. Next, he would "wash his heart with spirits," something like the alcohol doctors now rub on a patient's arm before giving an injection. On some mornings he would have to swallow a powder that he hated because it made him sick. Strangely enough, because superstitions still shaped parts of the practice of medicine, Wilhelm could obtain this powder only once per month, when the moon was waning. About a half hour after ingesting the powder he would take "a bit-ter essence" designed to make his stomach feel better and to make him feel like eating again. In the late morning he was supposed to take some more pills, before washing the area of his heart again between noon and two o'clock. Then more pills and the bitter essence to make him hungry. He then could eat a little before more pills and washing around four o'clock, with more of the same before going to bed at night. On top of all this, Reil had Wilhelm undergo the latest treatment—wearing a magnetic band around his heart.

As time went on, the professor also had Wilhelm bathe in the hot springs, holding a cool sponge over his heart. He also had him try another kind of pill, one that Wilhelm had to be careful handling because it would explode if it got too warm. But the strangest treatment was the electrical cure. The electric battery had been invented just nine years earlier, so this really was an experimental treatment. After the baths Wilhelm would go to the clinic, where the staff would wheel in a strange contraption that he described as a "magnificent, large mahogany machine." For ten minutes he would sit, bound with chains, on a stool on a glass-legged table while the electrical current passed through the chains. The current didn't bother him unless someone brushed against his coat; then sparks would crackle and flow out of him and he would feel a shock. Whatever the treatment's benefit, Wilhelm was impressed with Professor Reil, calling him a "wonderful man."

But he didn't stay impressed with the procedure. He soon wrote Jacob, telling him that he now received the electric shock treatments daily, but that they caused increasingly "unpleasant sensations." "On hot days," he wrote in late July, when it was often quite warm, the current "is so strong that blisters rise where the electrical connectors touch me." Moreover, he could hear other people "scream terribly" when receiving shocks from the machine.

What made Wilhelm's stay in Halle even harder was that while his physical heart was being treated, his emotional heart was being hurt. The long-distance relationship was hard on his friendship with Jacob. Letters could take a week or ten days to travel between Kassel and Halle, and misunderstandings had plenty of time to grow before they could be corrected. When Jacob wrote that he hadn't heard from Wilhelm for a long time and questioned when he was going to come home, Wilhelm thought that Jacob resented Wilhelm's expensive stay. When he defended himself, he hurt Jacob's feelings. "How could you put me in this position," Jacob wrote back dramatically, "when I just once spoke of your stay in Halle?" He asked Wilhelm if he ever wanted to come home again and whether Wilhelm believed that he loved him. That "scolding" was going too far, Wilhelm replied. How could Jacob "doubt his love for him"? Like Jacob, Wilhelm was dramatic in his response: "I'd give up my life if I had to . . . writing can't express my fondness for you."

While it might sound as if these treatments filled Wilhelm's days, apparently they didn't. When he wasn't submitting to one of Professor Reil's new ideas, Wilhelm had time to scour old books for folktales and folk songs, and he spent many evenings visiting with a local family who entertained many musicians and writers. The Grimms' friend Clemens Brentano also spent a month in Halle, staying in the same house with Wilhelm. Brentano had a good number of intriguing books with him, including a collection of Spanish folktales from the fifteenth century. Wilhelm eagerly copied them.

And so with pills and baths and books, the summer passed and, after almost six months of treatment, Wilhelm began feeling better, though we have to wonder if the improvement was really the result of the treatments. In September another friend, Achim von Arnim, invited Wilhelm and Brentano to visit him in Berlin. When Brentano promised to pay Wilhelm's way and to let him finish copying Brentano's books, Wilhelm accepted. Berlin was the capital of what, before Napoleon's invasion, had been Prussia. Although its streets were largely deserted and its palaces empty because the king was in exile, Wilhelm was impressed with the city. He wrote Tante Zimmer that "it is pleasant to be here, and this beautiful city is imposing to anybody who sees it for the first time."

Because Arnim introduced Wilhelm to many writers and artists, this trip was for him what the trip to Paris had been for Jacob. It opened his eyes to a larger world and perhaps helped him imagine himself contributing something to that world. It was after this visit to Berlin that Wilhelm had the courage to visit his hero, the famous writer Johann Wolfgang von Goethe, and to begin more energetically to contact writers and scholars from other countries.

But if Wilhelm's health was up to a busier social schedule, his wardrobe wasn't. Moreover, the autumn was bringing cooler temperatures. Since his friends were already paying for his trip, he didn't feel comfortable asking them for help with clothes. And so in October 1809, he wrote Jacob, asking him to inquire about the cost of sending a brown wool coat to Berlin. Others had told Wilhelm that sending it by post ought not to cost more than one taler, and Wilhelm was willing to spend that much. He also asked if Jacob had purchased some new silk underwear for himself; if so, Wilhelm wondered if Jacob would send him an old pair. Jacob replied that he had thrown away his old underclothes long before and advised Wilhelm to get some new ones made for himself. He did, however, send along a pair of wool pants.

December found Wilhelm back in Kassel, reunited with Jacob, who, having worried very much about Wilhelm's health, was overjoyed to see his brother. In some ways life was still not easy for the Grimms. French secret police were everywhere in the city, creating an atmosphere of suspicion and worry among the inhabitants. A person could not drop a candy wrapper, Wilhelm reported, but a member of the secret police would scoop it up to see if a message were scribbled inside. Moreover, household expenses and high taxes imposed by the French quickly ate up Jacob's income. But the brothers were happy to be able to live together again.

For the most part, Jacob's job at the palace library was routine. He cataloged books and copied manuscripts, sometimes borrowing items from other libraries for Wilhelm or himself. For the most part the king and queen didn't bother him. But one day the king decided to use the room that contained the library for something else. He ordered Jacob to carry all the books within thirty-six hours to an attic of another palace. Jacob met the deadline and, a short time later, had to move several thousand of the most valuable books to yet another part of the palace.

That decision very nearly brought tragedy into the brothers' lives. Late one Saturday night in November 1811, the first really cold night of the year—cold enough to make the streets freeze solid and to hang icicles from the eaves of the houses—Jacob and Wilhelm were awakened by bells ringing to announce a fire. Wilhelm got up quickly and looked out the front window of their house, only to see flames rising above the palace. Apparently, a new heating system had been poorly installed, and when it was used on this cold night, it started a fire, which spread so quickly that the king and queen barely escaped.

Jacob dressed at once and rushed to the scene. At home, as he watched the flames and the soldiers and civilians rushing to fight the blaze, Wilhelm worried desperately about Jacob. He knew that Jacob would take great risks to save his beloved books. His worry grew stronger when soldiers hurried past carrying a man who had been injured in the fire. And Wilhelm had reason to worry. Jacob had indeed rushed into the palace and, while everything around him was in flames, had wrapped books in linen sheets. With the help of some soldiers, he carried the books safely to the courtyard. Bringing them out from their new location was particularly difficult because Jacob had to descend a small winding staircase and feel around in the dark for the exit. Eventually, around five o'clock in the morning, forced out of the building by the smoke, Jacob returned home, his clothes filled with the acrid smell of the fire.

Wilhelm made some coffee while Jacob rested a little. Then, with the fire worsening and the wind now blowing toward the houses in Kassel, Jacob returned to the palace to care for the books he had left in the courtyard. Wilhelm and their sister, Lotte, got ready to flee in case the fire threatened their house. All the bells in the city were ringing, warning the citizens to be ready. The Grimms took water to their attic and Lotte gathered the keys to all their cupboards so that they could gather their valuables quickly. Wilhelm bundled up important papers. But with sunrise there came good news. Although the palace had been largely destroyed, the city was no longer in danger. The cold weather had been their savior. The heavy frost on the rooftops had prevented any sparks or embers from getting a start on the houses.

Many people took the fire as a sign of something more important. Some argued that it was a signal that the French government was going to collapse and burn, just as the palace had. Others suggested that it marked the end of one thousand years of Hessian rule in Hesse. From exile the count mourned the loss of the palace where he was born, and even King Jérôme was troubled by the loss of his throne room.

Jacob, apparently, understood the fire as a signal of hard work to come. "These," he would say later in a considerable understatement, "were not my most pleasant days." The books that he had to care for sat in a huge heap. Except for a small room already filled with glass ornaments, there was nowhere for Jacob to put them. In addition, the queen ordered Jacob to separate her books from the rest of the collection. For someone who loved nothing better than an orderly study, working in this chaos was torment.

Fortunately, Jacob had something of a sanctuary at home, where he and Wilhelm could continue, in a more peaceful setting, their study of old German literature. And increasingly as they studied during these years, their attention focused on the subject that would come to be associated with their name. They began writing about old literature and folktales in scholarly journals. In fact, back when Wilhelm was in Halle undergoing Professor Reil's treatments, he and Jacob had frequently asked in letters if the other had found any new fairy tales for children. They were eager to hear the words "Once upon a time."

CHAPTER FIVE

Collecting the Tales

After they had eaten and drunk, the dwarf said, "Since you have such a good heart and gladly share what you have, I'm going to grant you some good luck. There's an old tree over there. Just go and chop it down, and you'll find something among the roots." Then the dwarf took leave of him.

Simpleton went over and chopped down the tree. When it fell, he saw a goose with feathers of pure gold lying among the roots.

—THE GOLDEN GOOSE

It is perhaps not surprising—with the French controlling the government and Napoleon's brother and his queen ordering Jacob to carry books first here, then there—that he and Wilhelm retreated to their desks to study German stories. Imagine how strange it must have been to be forced to stop speaking the language they had grown up with and to speak another language. Imagine how frustrating it must have been for people who loved their cultural heritage to watch the French pack up paintings and books to send to France as spoils of war. And, indeed, Wilhelm would admit that "the eagerness" with which they "pushed" toward their studies "helped to surmount the oppression of those days."

But the brothers' search for German folktales was more than an attempt to forget what was going on around them. "Without a doubt," Wilhelm said, "the world events and our need for peace in scholarship contributed to the awakening of this long-forgotten literature." They "didn't only seek comfort in the past," however, but "hoped naturally that this direction could contribute to the return of a different time." They collected the fairy tales because they hoped the stories would help remind their countrymen of what it meant to be German. Every person, they said, who "journeys out into life" is "accompanied by a good angel." This angelic "companion" is "none other than the inexhaustible store of tales, legends, and history, all of which coexist and strive to bring us closer to the refreshing and invigorating spirit of earlier ages."

The hard part of collecting the fairy tales was finding them, for these weren't the kinds of stories that Jacob had seen when he worked in the library in Paris with Savigny or that Wilhelm had hunted up in old bookstores in Kassel or Halle. Nor were they the kinds of stories that the brothers had written about in articles for magazines. Rather, these were stories that their mother had told them as boys while they were sitting at the kitchen table or while she was putting them to bed. These were stories that people just told; they never thought to write them down.

In France a hundred years earlier Charles Perrault had collected eight French tales, including "Cinderella," "Little Red Riding Hood," and "Puss in Boots," for the children of the nobles. But Jacob and Wilhelm weren't very impressed with his *Tales from Mother Goose*. Part of the problem was the language. They admired the simple way Perrault told the tales, but they thought that "there is really nothing more difficult than using the French language to tell children's stories . . . without pretentiousness."

Jacob and Wilhelm weren't the first people to think about preserving the German fairy tales. They were the first, however, to attack the job seriously. Other writers had used the tales for their own purposes. Some fifteen years earlier Johann Ludwig Tieck had published a book titled simply *Folktales,* but he used the tales to tell jokes and to criticize society. Others used parts of traditional fairy tales as stepping stones to tell their own stories. In 1805 the brothers' friends Achim von Arnim and Clemens Brentano published a challenge in their book *The Boy's Magic Horn* for writers to save folktales and songs. The new generation was not telling stories and singing songs the way previous generations had, and these writers were afraid that this oral German heritage would be lost. Now Jacob and Wilhelm were ready to accept the challenge.

The brothers got more excited about the challenge when Arnim received copies of two fairy tales that had been collected by an artist named Philipp Otto Runge. Runge had heard the stories from fishermen and had tried to take them down word for word. Anyone who made a collection of these stories, Runge wrote in a letter, would find it worthwhile and rewarding work. Arnim passed both stories on to the Grimms. He published "The Juniper Tree" in a newspaper that he put out, and on one of his visits to Kassel he brought "The Fisherman and His Wife" for the brothers to copy. The Grimms would use both of these in their collection, and they would also be inspired to follow Runge's example of collecting stories from living storytellers whenever possible.

As the Grimms explained in the foreword to their book, they believed that their collection came at a crucial moment:

It is probably just the right time to collect these tales, since those who have been preserving them are becoming ever harder to find (to be sure, those who still know them know a great deal, because people may die, but the stories live on). The custom of telling tales is ever on the wane, just as all the cozy corners in homes and in gardens are giving way to an empty splendor that resembles the smile with which one speaks of these tales — a smile that looks elegant but costs so little. Where they still exist, the tales live on in such a way that no one thinks about whether they are good or bad, poetic or vulgar. We know them and love them just because we happen to have heard them a certain way, and we like them without reflecting why.

But if storytellers were becoming scarcer, Jacob and Wilhelm did not have to travel far to find some good sources of tales. To begin with, they had only to look next door, to the household of the Wild family. Herr Wild was an apothecary, or druggist, an occupation that naturally put him in contact with a lot of people. Frau Wild and four of their six daughters—Gretchen, Lisette, Marie, and Dorothea—loved storytelling. Lotte Grimm was the same age as Dorothea, whom everyone called Dortchen, and the two friends found many good stories for Lotte's older brothers.

Wilhelm found something else in Dortchen—his life's true love—and though he didn't marry her until fourteen years later, their friendship certainly grew as Dortchen passed on some of the fairy tales she knew. The Wilds, like many residents of Kassel, kept a garden outside the city limits. Sometimes Dortchen, Lotte, and Wilhelm would walk out to their plot and tell stories in the

Wilds' small garden house. Even when it was cold, the friends would use the garden house for a meeting place. Wilhelm's notes on the fairy tales tell us, for example, that in January 1812, Dortchen told him the story of "The Singing Bone" while they were gathered around "the stove in the summer-house."

Historians disagree about the role of another member of the Wild household—the family's nanny and housekeeper, Marie Müller, whom they affectionately called "Old Marie." Marie's husband, a blacksmith, had been one of the Hessian soldiers who had gone to America during the Revolutionary War to help the British fight against George Washington's troops. After her husband was killed in the New World, she needed a way to support herself and so came to work for the Wilds. Some historians believe Wilhelm's son Herman, who said that Old Marie contributed several important tales, including "Little Red Cap"; others think that a younger woman named Marie, from a different family, was responsible for these tales.

The brothers also asked their friends for help in collecting the tales. Jacob wrote to Paul Wigand, who had become a magistrate in a village just north of Kassel. Since a magistrate saw everyone who got in trouble with the law, Jacob urged him to "examine all rascals and thieves," listening carefully to the testimony for any good "robber songs, superstitions, or sayings" and writing them down exactly as they were spoken. Jacob also reminded him that farmers, fishermen, coal burners, and old peasant women were good resources for material. However, Paul didn't come up with much for the brothers.

Other friends were more productive. In fact, a book club that met every Friday evening to discuss what the members were reading was quick to help out. The brothers' friends from the lyceum, Ernst von der Malsburg and Fritz von Schwertzell, weren't particularly helpful, but Friedericke Mannel, a country girl, whose father was the pastor of a church not far away, furnished a couple of tales, and two sisters, Amalie and Jeanette Hassenpflug, whose father was an important politician in the city, came up with about a dozen stories, including "Brier Rose," "Tom Thumb," and "Snow White," which would be among the most famous. Since Amalie and Jeanette's mother was descended from a French family, some of the stories that the girls knew had been influenced by Charles Perrault's tales, which Jacob and Wilhelm didn't realize right away. Thus, they included a version of the Frenchman's "Puss in Boots" that the Hassenpflugs had told them. Later, in the second edition of their fairy tales, they took it out because they wanted their collection to be made entirely of fairy tales with a German heritage.

Jacob and Wilhelm also wanted their collection to be as accurate and complete as possible, and so they were a little wary of relying only on friends and neighbors for help. In January 1811 Jacob prepared an invitation to be sent throughout Hesse that described what he and Wilhelm were looking for. He asked for local tales or legends, particularly those that were told to children or were told in the spinning room in winter. It didn't matter, Jacob said, if the stories taught a lesson or were just fun to listen to, whether they were happy or sad. What was important was that the person writing down the story should capture every word the teller said, even if the story didn't make sense the way that it was told.

One person who responded to the invitation was Ferdinand

Siebert. He was the son of a teacher and heard lots of tales, he told Wilhelm, from his father's students and from the peasant families whom he worked with during the summers. Ferdinand contributed several stories, and it's not hard to imagine the country schoolboys enjoying the tale of "The Brave Little Tailor," about a tailor who pretends to be a mighty warrior and then actually becomes a giant killer. Unfortunately, the Grimms couldn't use all the tales Ferdinand provided because some of them had been "corrected" by the schoolboys. Their use of "proper" German robbed the tales of their charm.

Although some modern books and videos about the Grimms suggest that they relentlessly combed the countryside for stories, the brothers actually made few trips. Some trips paid off, as when Wilhelm, on a visit to Höxter, where Paul Wigand lived, met a shepherd who could furnish some tales. Others were not so successful. Both Lotte and Wilhelm made separate trips to Marburg to meet with Frau Creuzer, an old woman who, they had heard, was a great source of stories. The more they asked Frau Creuzer about fairy tales, however, the more she insisted that she didn't know any stories. She was afraid that Wilhelm would give her a bad name and make her a laughingstock.

Wilhelm wasn't willing to give up. He was certain from what he had been told that Frau Creuzer knew many wonderful tales. Finally, he hit upon a plan. Because of a long-term illness Frau Creuzer was living in a Marburg hospital. Wilhelm convinced the superintendent of the hospital to take his children to visit her and then, when she told her tales to the children, the superintendent could write them down for Wilhelm.

Jacob and Wilhelm had better luck with an old soldier named

Johann Friedrich Krause, a former sergeant-major who had no doubt swapped many a tale in his soldiering days. Krause now swapped a few stories for some of Jacob and Wilhelm's old pants. He would tell them a story, and they would give him their old trousers. We have to wonder if the old soldier had himself in mind when he told the brothers about "Old Sultan," a dog so old and useless that he was going to be shot—even his loyalty to his master couldn't save him. And Krause must have wished that he had the kind of magical items that were featured in "The Knapsack, the Hat, and the Horn," another story that he told, because, like many old soldiers, he had a hard time supporting himself after the war. For several years Krause periodically wrote to Jacob and Wilhelm, telling the brothers that he thought of them daily—morning and evening as he dressed and undressed—and then asking if either of them had another pair of old trousers to pass along, because his were now worn out.

And so by means of tricks and trades, gifts and gatherings, the collection of tales grew. But even as they were seeking out fairy tales, both brothers were finishing other projects as well. In 1811 each of them published his first book. Jacob's was a scholarly book about the German mastersingers, who from the 1300s through the 1500s composed songs for the nobles and the rulers. Wilhelm's was a translation of Danish songs and poems of chivalry, stories of knights and love and honor. Both Jacob and Wilhelm were fascinated by the similarities between old Scandinavian literature and old German literature.

Clemens Brentano had been one of the early supporters of the fairy tale project, but as Jacob and Wilhelm pressed on with their collection, he almost came into competition with them. First, he started translating a collection of Italian fairy tales into German, something that was different enough from Jacob and Wilhelm's project that it wouldn't hurt the sales of their fairy tales. But then, when he tired of working on the translation, Brentano decided to put together a book of German fairy tales just like the one the Grimms were doing.

Jacob and Wilhelm didn't try to stop him. They believed that friendship was more important than professional success. When he asked to use some of the tales that they had collected, Wilhelm's reply was gracious. "All that we have is as much yours as ours," he wrote, "and you can look through our children's stories when you are in Kassel." They remembered the ways that Brentano had entertained them and helped them when they were students in Marburg and when Wilhelm was sick in Halle. Jacob agreed with Wilhelm's generosity. "Clemens is heartily welcome to our collection," Jacob said. "It would be petty of us not to repay in such a small way his kindness, even if his way of working is not ours."

Indeed, Brentano's way of working was not like Jacob and Wilhelm's. What Jacob meant was that whereas the Grimms worked hard for accuracy, trying to get every phrase just as the storyteller spun the tale, Brentano was more relaxed. He would take hasty notes when listening to a story and then write it down later in his own words, using his own imagination freely to add to the tale. But in other ways, too, Brentano worked differently from Jacob and Wilhelm. Where they were disciplined and organized, he was sloppy and undisciplined. It turned out that the reason Frau Creuzer wouldn't tell her stories to the Grimms initially was that Brentano had been to see her first and that he had somehow made her distrustful of people collecting tales.

Fortunately for us, Jacob and Wilhelm copied their manuscript before they lent it to Brentano. If they hadn't, we might not know the Grimms' fairy tales the way we do today. Jacob and Wilhelm gave Brentano the manuscript with the understanding that he would return it, but he never did. No one knows exactly what happened to it. It simply disappeared for almost a hundred years until it reappeared in 1920 in the library of the Abbey of Oelenberg, in the part of northern France that shares a border with Germany. Not surprisingly, the relationship between the Grimms and Brentano became a bit strained, although the brothers seemed more impatient with Brentano than angry. Brentano appears to have been the one to disrupt the friendship. When Jacob and Wilhelm sent him copies of the books they published in 1811, he never acknowledged receiving them. Their paths would continue to cross over the next ten years, but what spark of friendship there had once been was never rekindled.

The Grimms kept adding to their manuscript, editing it and making changes, comparing different versions of the same tales and selecting the version they believed to be the most authentic, until they had thirty-seven more tales than they had sent Brentano. Achim von Arnim, who with Brentano had encouraged them to collect the fairy tales, watched their progress from a distance. Despite Brentano's lack of interest in supporting Jacob and Wilhelm, Arnim was still intrigued by their project, but he was worried that the brothers were being perfectionists and that they would never think that their manuscript was finished enough to publish. Finally, in January 1812 Arnim visited Kassel to look it over.

As Wilhelm watched, Arnim paced back and forth across the

room, flipping through the sheets of paper as he read the tales. All the while a tame canary perched calmly on the top of his head, now and then gracefully moving its wings for balance but appearing, Wilhelm said, "to be quite at home amidst his thick locks." Perhaps Wilhelm's heart was something like that bird, balancing between pride and anxiety as his and Jacob's hopes rested on Arnim's head.

But if Wilhelm was at all worried, he need not have been. Arnim loved the manuscript and eagerly set off for Berlin to find a publisher for it. As much as they believed in their friend, Jacob and Wilhelm couldn't be sure that he would succeed in his task. Book sales were slow in the second decade of the nineteenth century, and publishers as a result were slow to take on new projects. But with the help of Ferdinand Dümmler, another writer and a friend of the Grimms, Arnim convinced Georg Andreas Reimer, Dümmler's publisher, to publish the fairy tales.

That fall Jacob and Wilhelm sent off to Berlin what would become the first volume of their collection—eighty-six stories in all. Even though they clearly saw the fairy tales as children's stories, they didn't make this first edition of the collection very appealing to children. There were no illustrations, but there were footnotes and a long introduction that explained what the Grimms thought about the fairy tales.

While both brothers had collected the stories (about half of the tales in the manuscript that Brentano lost were in Jacob's handwriting and half in Wilhelm's), Wilhelm seems to have written the introduction by himself. Perhaps the fact that it was fall put the image of harvests in his mind, because that's how he portrayed the collection. The tales were like the few stalks of a crop that managed to survive "a storm or some other mishap sent by heaven," he wrote. Then, "at the end of the summer, once they have ripened and become full, poor devout hands come to seek them out; ear upon ear, carefully bound and esteemed more highly than entire sheaves, they are carried home, and for the entire winter, they provide nourishment, perhaps the only seed for the future."

In December 1812, just five days before Christmas, the harvest that had been gathered by the hands of the "poor devout" brothers was sent forth to households all over Germany. The book, *Kinder- und Hausmärchen* or *Children's and Household Tales,* was dedicated "To Frau Elisabeth von Arnim, for the little Johannes Freimund." In the nineteenth century, someone who really liked a particular book would have it bound in special leather covers. That's what Achim von Arnim did for his wife, Elisabeth, Clemens Brentano's sister, who was known to her friends as Bettina and who would come to be one of the Grimms' strongest supporters. On Christmas she found it, bound in green leather with gold lettering and edging, waiting for her on the table. She was delighted with the present and the chivalrous dedication from the Grimms to her and her son.

What the world would think of the fairy tales was another matter. Wilhelm hoped that people would receive them favorably. He concluded the preface to the book with these words: "We bequeath this book to well-meaning hands and cannot help but think of the powerful blessing that dwells in them. We hope that the book will remain completely unknown to those who begrudge poor and modest souls these small morsels of poetry."

CHAPTER SIX

The Fairy Tale Road

*She walked about searching for a way out but could find none.
When evening came, she sat under a tree, commended herself to
God, and planned to remain there no matter what might happen.
But after she had been sitting there awhile, a white dove came
flying to her with a little golden key in its beak. It put the key in
her hand and said, "Do you see that large tree over there? You'll
find a little lock on it, and if you open it with this key, you'll find
plenty of food in it and you won't have to go hungry anymore."*

—THE OLD WOMAN IN THE FOREST

The fairy tales," wrote Joseph von Görres, a friend of the
Grimms and an important newspaper editor from Koblenz,
"impatiently awaited by my children, have now arrived and we
have not been able to tear them from the children's hands. My
youngest girl, Arnim's godchild, can already recite some of the stories, particularly those with rhymes. My eldest girl has spread
them among the children in the town."

Such responses were music to Jacob and Wilhelm's ears. And,
indeed, many people sang the praises of their work. One admirer
even suggested that it was as important as Martin Luther's translation of the Bible into German, which had been published in the
1520s. And although the publisher of the fairy tales didn't adver-

tise them, he was able to sell all nine hundred copies within three years.

But not everyone thought that Jacob and Wilhelm were on the same level as Martin Luther. Brentano complained that there were too many fairy tales of the same type. One critic wrote that most of the book was "sheer trash." In Austria, *Household Tales* was banned because of its "superstitious" content.

Even Arnim, who had supported the book, wondered whether it was appropriate for children. One mother, he said, wouldn't let her children touch the book because of the tale "How Some Children Played at Slaughtering," which appeared in two brief versions. Wilhelm was quick to defend the story, in which children, pretending to butcher pigs, actually kill playmates. His own mother, Wilhelm said, had told them the story when they were children, and it had made him play more carefully. It was not too different from parts of the Bible, he argued, which had been read to him and Jacob every night without any ill effect.

Arnim also thought that some of the tales about husbands and wives were too mature for children and that illustrations were more important than footnotes for young readers. Wilhelm agreed, but Jacob's response to Arnim reveals what was a growing difference of opinion between the brothers. "My book was not written for children," he said, "though it fills a need for them, and I am glad that this should be so." More important was the book's value as "a source of poetry, mythology, and history." Because it preserved a bit of old German culture, Jacob thought that the book should be "for the oldest and most serious of people."

Despite these differences of opinion, the publisher was eager for another volume of tales, and Jacob and Wilhelm kept on collecting. The second volume grew even more quickly than the first had. "This was," Wilhelm said when it was published, "in part because it had earned itself friends who supported it, in part because those who would have liked to support it earlier now clearly perceived the what and how of it." And if it looked as if they were lucky, Wilhelm said, they were, but it was the kind of luck that might appear accidental but that came from "diligent, persevering" effort. "Once you become accustomed to looking out for something, you find it far more frequently than can be imagined."

One such piece of luck was that they met a peasant woman from a village on the outskirts of Kassel. Dorothea Viehmann, who came to be known as "the Fairy Tale Wife," passed on thirty-five stories to the Grimms, half of the tales that would be published in the second volume. The Viehmanns were poor in possessions, having lost everything they owned in a battle between Hessians and King Jérôme's soldiers, but they were rich in stories. Frau Viehmann was a perfect source for the brothers, who were as concerned about accuracy as she was about telling a good tale.

"She had the old stories clearly in mind," Wilhelm wrote later, "and she herself said that not everyone had this gift and that most people could not keep things in the right order. She narrated carefully, confidently, and in an unusually lively manner, taking pleasure in it. At first she spoke spontaneously, then, if one asked, she repeated what she had said slowly so that, with a little practice, it could be transcribed." Anyone who doubts the accuracy of the oral tradition, he said, or anyone who thinks that storytellers make up the tales "should have the chance to hear how precisely she stays with each story and how keen she is to narrate it correctly. When she retells something, she never changes its substance and

Dorothea Viehmann, source of much of the second volume of Household Tales

corrects an error as soon as she notices it, even if it means inter-rupting herself."

As time went on, collecting the fairy tales fell more and more to Wilhelm. In part this was because of what was happening in the world around them. During December 1812, when the Grimms were celebrating the publication of the fairy tales, Napoleon and his armies were losing their battle to conquer Russia. Instead of adding Russia to his empire, Napoleon was being chased back into western Europe. Of the more than 450,000 soldiers he had led into Russia, only 40,000 returned.

The tide was turning against Napoleon, and King Jérôme knew it. He had started to follow his brother into Russia but had turned back after the two of them argued. As Napoleon retreated into Prussia and the German kingdoms, the summer of 1813 was filled with battles and the rumors of battles. Jérôme saw the "Grand Army" trying to live off cabbage stems and moldy bread. The future did not look good for the emperor. Jérôme prepared to flee, and he ordered Jacob, who was still his librarian, to pack books and art treasures to carry with him to France.

Sending rare Hessian books and manuscripts out of the country was the last thing Jacob wanted to do, but he had no choice. He knew enough to take the order seriously. All too often that summer soldiers who had been caught trying to desert from the army were led past his window on their way to be executed. To save as many irreplaceable manuscripts as he could, he tried to trick the French by convincing Jérôme's court that they weren't worth taking with them.

While Jacob was trying to save those old Hessian books, Wilhelm was trying to save more fairy tales. As he made the short trip to an estate near Paderborn that was owned by friends, the Haxthausens, Wilhelm must have felt that he was going back in time as well as away from the war. The Haxthausens were a family who loved old German customs. They told stories and sang folk songs together and wore traditional folk clothing. Visiting them was always an adventure because of the roads. On his first visit Wilhelm hired a horse cart, but after it turned over twice, he decided to make the trip on foot. This time a boar hunt as well as the rough road held him up, and the carriage driver quit.

But when he finally made it to the Haxthausens' estate, he found the effort more than worth his while. The Haxthausens' daughters, Anna and Ludowine, became enthusiastic collectors of tales. People trusted the young girls more than they might adults and freely told them stories to pass on to Wilhelm. The girls continued collecting even after Wilhelm left and finally, the next winter, sent him their treasure, thoughtfully copied into an album embroidered with pearls. They would provide twenty of the seventy tales for the second volume.

During his visit, Wilhelm met someone who, some people claim, was his first true love. Eighteen-year-old Jenny von Droste-Hülshoff and her younger sister, Annette, were the nieces of the Haxthausen girls, but because they were close in age, they were also their good friends. Wilhelm later wrote Jacob that Jenny was charming and quiet, and Jenny was apparently quite struck by Wilhelm as well. "Wilhelm kissed Nette's hand," she told her diary, "and then mine, but we did not speak; at that moment my mind was quite blank, and if he had said anything I would not have understood." On other occasions, Jenny confessed to her diary that she was angry when Wilhelm kissed the hands of her sisters and talked too long with them.

Annette, who later became a famous poet, seems to have made a different impression on Wilhelm. He told Jacob she was "pushy and unpleasant," entirely the opposite of Jenny. The following January, Wilhelm wrote Ludowine von Haxthausen that he "recently had a strange and frightening dream about Fräulein Nette." Wrapped in "dark purple flames, she pulled single hairs from her head and threw them into the air toward me. They turned into arrows and could easily have blinded me, had it all been in earnest."

Wilhelm and Jenny kept up their friendship, sending gifts and talking fondly of each other, but for some reason they never became engaged. Some people think that social class got in the way. Jenny was from an aristocratic family, while Wilhelm was an unemployed scholar the summer they met. Other people suggest that religion was the barrier to their love, because Jenny was devoted to the Roman Catholic Church and Wilhelm was devoted to the Calvinist Reformed Church, which had split from the Catholic Church during the Reformation. Many of the wars of the prior two hundred years had been fought because of differences among Catholics, Lutherans, and Calvinists, and feelings were still strong. But whatever the causes of their separation, Wilhelm and Jenny shared their thoughts if not their lives, writing letters to each other for more than twenty years, even after Wilhelm had married, until, at the age of forty, Jenny married a baron who was considerably older than she was.

It wasn't possible, of course, to truly forget the war, even in the almost ideal world of the Haxthausens' country estate. The Haxthausen brothers, Werner and August, through whom Jacob and Wilhelm had met the family originally, were both affected by the fighting. It was Werner, forced into exile in Sweden and England because of his anti-French activities, who through letters had helped to arrange Wilhelm's visit.

August, on the other hand, had joined the army, hoping to liberate Germany. Yet even in the midst of fighting, he took time to record stories for his friends. He sent Wilhelm "The Crows," a tale told him by a fellow soldier while the two of them were on sentry duty. This gloomy story about two soldiers who are picked to death by crows seemed all the sadder to Wilhelm because the soldier who told it to August was killed three days later.

Back at home that October, Jacob woke up one morning to

the sound of wagons and carriages rumbling past his window. Jérôme and the French were fleeing. Westphalians—Germans who had collaborated with the French—still controlled Kassel, but Russian troops were camped around the city. The residents of Kassel got ready for a battle, gathering jewels and family treasures in case they had to evacuate. Jacob and Wilhelm packed up their treasures—the manuscripts of the fairy tales and other important letters and papers.

Many of the Westphalian soldiers deserted, unwilling to fight for the losing French cause. A good number of the "defenders" of the city were teenage boys forced into service or taken from military schools. When the more experienced Russian soldiers captured one such unit, they took away their uniforms as well as their guns. Dressed only in their tall blue hats, these young Westphalian soldiers were marched to Kassel from the scene of the battle. There the boys hid in a guardhouse until they could get some clothes to wear.

When the carts that had been used to barricade the city gates were pulled out of the way, a Russian general by the name of Czernitshev pranced into Kassel on a horse as excited citizens tried to hug him and his horse. Other residents danced in the streets to welcome the Russians who were liberating them. Prince Wilhelm, heir to the Hessian throne, was met at the city gates by children singing hymns. The conquering soldiers needed places to stay, and the people of Kassel opened their houses. Jacob and Wilhelm had seven Russian soldiers stay with them. Despite their knowledge of several languages, the brothers did not understand Russian. They were amazed at the habits of the Russians, particularly their great capacity for eating and drinking as well as their singing and dancing. As hard as it must have been to concentrate, however, Wilhelm kept working on the fairy tale collection, often writing while the soldiers were singing in the next room.

After almost a month Kassel was ready for its exiled ruler, Count Wilhelm, to return, and when his carriage entered the streets, which had been decorated with wildflowers, the towns-people—including Jacob and Wilhelm—cheered his arrival. A ruler like the count never traveled alone, so behind his open carriage came the carriages of his court—gentlemen and ladies-in-waiting and advisers. When they saw the countess and her loyal lady-in-waiting, Tante Zimmer, Jacob and Wilhelm were overjoyed and ran alongside the carriage, calling out greetings.

"In those months," Jacob later recalled, "everything was in excited motion." Once again Hesse would be ruled by Hessians, and German would be the language of the land. But although King Jérôme was gone, Napoleon wasn't finished fighting. To help the cause, the brothers dedicated the profits from another book project to the Hessian army. The book, *Poor Heinrich*, fit the situation, they thought. It was a long poem about a knight and a maiden who make great sacrifices, the kinds of sacrifices that the Grimms believed they now needed to make.

The family ended up contributing a lot to the support of their country. First, Jacob and Wilhelm's younger brothers, Carl and Ludwig, joined the Hessian army, and then Jacob was called back into official service. When the Westphalian government dissolved, so did Jacob's job as court librarian, but in December 1813 he was offered a job in the Hessian government as secretary to the diplomats being sent to Paris to negotiate the peace.

Leaving Wilhelm to work on the fairy tales, Jacob set off once again for Paris. His route this time was not as direct as on the previous trip. The delegation followed the fighting and the sounds of guns south along the border of France and Germany into Switzerland and back into France, staying just behind the battles. That made for some danger and excitement. In Frankfurt, Russian soldiers on a looting binge hit the inn where the group was staying, robbing a Prussian official of his horses and almost taking Jacob's luggage. That might not have been so bad, because, as Jacob wrote Wilhelm, Lotte had packed his worst black silk trousers, leaving his good pair at home. Although Jacob was bored by riding in a coach with Count Keller, the leader of the diplomatic mission, who loved to talk about life at court and gossip about the families of nobles, sometimes the travelers had to hurriedly change direction to escape danger or pass burning villages with dead horses and dead soldiers along the road.

One way that Jacob dealt with the boredom and the horror was to hunt for collections of books or art in the cities through which they passed. He met a number of other book lovers on the journey and

Carl Grimm in the uniform of the Hessian cavalry, 1814

always asked whether they knew about *Household Tales*, and he wrote letters to people like Sir Walter Scott in Scotland, asking about fairy tales from their countries. He also wrote Wilhelm long letters, of course, sending him the latest political news as well as reports about the paintings and books, cathedrals and glockenspiels (musical bell towers, sometimes with carved figures that move) that he encountered.

Although he was in the midst of some of the most exciting events in Europe, Jacob missed home. He wrote to his brother that he dreamed about him at night and that, in those moments in the carriage when he would go back and forth between sleep and waking every ten minutes, he often awoke thinking he was in Kassel.

Lotte Grimm in 1821

Wilhelm wrote back to Jacob, assuring him that his desk and chairs and a peaceful life awaited him as soon as the fighting stopped. Wilhelm almost had to send Jacob some bad news. The chimney had caught fire, but before the house itself started burning, Wilhelm smothered the fire in the stove with a damp cloth. He also reported to Jacob on the progress of his writing.

Writing was never very far from either brother's mind. In Paris, Jacob spent any spare moments in the national library, searching for what he and Wilhelm treasured. He was especially excited about an old version of "Reynard the Fox" in Latin. His official job also involved looking for treasures—those carried off by the French during the occupation. The job was often thankless, but Jacob had one wonderful moment when he met the assistant whom King Jérôme had assigned to Jacob back in Kassel to help him pack Hessian treasures to send to France. The man's eyes grew big, Jacob reported, when he realized that Jacob was there to return the items to Hesse.

Money continued to be an issue for Jacob and Wilhelm. Part of the problem was that the government didn't pay all the expenses of its employees. Living in Paris was so expensive that Jacob had to ask for a raise in pay. Wilhelm, moreover, struggling to make ends meet in Kassel, had to come up with money for Ludwig's and Carl's uniforms, since the army didn't cover their cost.

Wilhelm felt bad that he didn't have a job that brought in more money, so when he heard that there might be an opening for a librarian's position similar to the one Jacob had had, he was eager to apply. A friend at court warned him, however, that the count was likely to reject an application for a full-time librarian because he didn't want to pay a full salary, so Wilhelm applied as the secretary to the librarian. His application letter shows just how much power the count still had. Wilhelm acknowledged the "gracious permission" that the count had given him to go to Marburg University. In case the count wondered what Wilhelm had been doing since the university, he explained that the "unhappy French occupation" had prevented him from applying for a position earlier and that he had occupied himself with scholarship. He now wanted to bring his "meager strengths" to serve his fatherland. Wilhelm knew that his first duty was to "go against the foes in the war," but since he couldn't do that because of illness, he now was requesting a place in the count's administration where he "would strive to serve with loyalty equal to that of his ancestors."

After making such promises, Wilhelm was granted the position, but he was disappointed to find that it paid only 100 talers per year. The family's part of the bill for Ludwig's uniform alone would take one third of Wilhelm's yearly salary.

Nor was the job as stimulating as Wilhelm had hoped. The library was open only three hours a day, and the public seemed reluctant about using it. Some residents would come in and ask how many books the library had and then leave without looking at any of them. In fact, the most popular reason for townspeople to visit was to see the spot where a Russian cannonball had crashed into the reading room. Just as Jacob had a few years before, Wilhelm used his spare time to study and write, so the collection of fairy tales continued to grow.

Late in the summer of 1814, while Wilhelm was finishing the collection, Jacob was sent on another diplomatic mission, this time to Vienna, Austria, south and east of Hesse. There the leaders of Europe were meeting to redefine their countries' borders after the war with Napoleon. Jacob's job at the conference, which was known as the Congress of Vienna, was to translate and write documents as the Hessian delegation met with Czar Alexander I of Russia and King Frederick William III of Prussia, as well as nobles and princes from Austria, Germany, and Great Britain.

Jacob wasn't that impressed with these participants, however. He wrote to Wilhelm: "Of the Congress, there is not much good to report: (1) nothing happens; or (2) what does is underhanded, petty, vulgar and moribund as if no great days lay ahead." Jacob was frustrated because, as he saw it, "our urgent basic needs are so clear that a little child could lead us on the right path," yet the princes and ministers of Europe let one silly question lead to another until the obvious points were hidden. The Prussians tried to argue that Prussians and Austrians weren't German. "So," Jacob complained, "the Berliner is not a German, but the citizens of Magdeburg and Münster presumably are." He also thought it was obvious that Poland, lying between Germany and Russia, ought to be a free country, but others wanted to divide it up. "The Congress," said one prince, "dances a lot, but does not advance." Jacob would have agreed.

Jacob's problems had begun on the five-day boat ride down the Danube River to Vienna. He had had to share a small room with two counts and a prince to whom he didn't enjoy talking. The accommodations weren't very noble. They had to sleep on hard benches without blankets, and Jacob caught a cold. In addition, Count Keller had rented a house in the suburbs of Vienna, requiring a ten-minute walk through dust and wind to get to the city. But perhaps worst of all, from Jacob's perspective, the Vienna libraries refused to let him check out books or manuscripts. Reading them there was fine, but Jacob, of course, had too little time to do that. Nonetheless, Wilhelm heard a rumor that Count Wilhelm in Kassel thought Jacob was spending too much time on his own interests and not enough time "in society." Jacob responded that while he didn't attend the parties, he was doing more than his share of the copying and translating. Still, this controversy added to his dislike of government service.

Jacob's one consolation was his association with other writers and book lovers. A group of them met every Wednesday night at a pub and talked about literature and fairy tales while eating a roast and drinking "poor beer and wine."

Wilhelm would have enjoyed such social hours. Back in Kassel, Ludwig had come home from the war and was good company, Wilhelm said, but it was clear that Wilhelm missed the companionship of his older brother. The Grimms and Tante Zimmer had celebrated Jacob's thirtieth birthday without him, and if that wasn't sad enough in itself, Wilhelm was depressed by the news of Jacob's unhappiness in his position. "If only the Congress were in Frankfurt," Wilhelm wrote, "I could visit you once in a while."

DOUBTING GIRL

A young girl once came to the Grimms carrying their book of fairy tales under her arm. When she met the brothers, she asked if she could read to them. According to Wilhelm, she did a very good job of reading the tale that ends with the words "and whoever does not believe this must pay a taler."

"As I do not believe it," she said, "I must pay you a taler. But since I don't have much pocket money, I can't pay you all at once."

With this, the girl opened a little pink purse, took out a groschen, and handed it to Wilhelm. When he tried to return it to her, she said, "Mama says that one must not accept money as a present."

Jacob's frustration with his situation occasionally made him pout in letters to Wilhelm. Even though he knew that the mail could be very irregular, Jacob chided Wilhelm for making him wait so long for letters. Wilhelm, who was writing just as regularly as Jacob, would patiently list the dates of the letters he had sent, reminding him that letters sent more recently could arrive before those sent earlier. But it must have been a little hard for Wilhelm to read Jacob's first reaction to volume two of *Household Tales*, which Wilhelm had sent to his brother in January 1815.

Near the end of a letter, without saying that it was good to see it in print or that he was happy that it was finished, Jacob simply noted that he had finally received it. "The paper and print are much worse," and the book is "thinner" and too high priced. Moreover, "you didn't put in all the notes," Jacob wrote, observing that there was room "after my last endnote." After asking Wilhelm to send a sample copy to someone in Frankfurt, Jacob went on to say that he was "looking forward to the third volume, for which I have prepared three or four new good long tales, as well as various fragments."

Wilhelm was perhaps used to Jacob's bluntness; there is no record of a response to his brother's criticisms. And while the two did keep collecting and revising fairy tales, sometimes adding new tales in subsequent editions, they would never publish a third volume. Part of the problem, perhaps, was that this second volume did not sell as well as the first. Money was tight because of the war, and book sales in general were not very good. The tales that Jacob collected while in Vienna, however, later grew into a discussion about the history of folktales that was printed as a long (more than two hundred pages!) series of notes in a later edition of *Household Tales*.

Despite differences in their personalities, the brothers remained close even during this almost-two-year separation. During the spring of 1815 that sense of closeness was intensified by a family tragedy. In April, Jacob opened a letter from Wilhelm only to read these words: "Oh, God, dearest Jacob, with what brokenheartedness I write you! This morning after nine o'clock . . . the good Lord took our favorite, most-loved aunt."

Tante Zimmer's death joined them closer together than ever, Jacob replied, because they had so few remaining relatives. Her death also made the brothers think seriously about life and death. Life seemed so fleeting, so temporary. Despite "all our love, sorrow, and trouble we can, in so few years, sink into a heap of earth," Jacob reminded Wilhelm. Such feelings guided them over the rest of their lives as they made decisions about where to live and work. Rarely again would they be separated.

CHAPTER SEVEN

Legends and Counts

Later on they boarded a ship and sailed across the sea. During the
trip the two older brothers plotted together against their brother.
"The youngest found the Water of Life, and we are empty-handed.
So our father will give him the kingdom that is ours by right, and
our brother will deprive us of our happiness."

Overcome by a desire for revenge, they planned how to put an
end to their brother.

—THE WATER OF LIFE

Jacob returned from Vienna in the summer of 1815, and though
it is not known whether he remembered to bring some seeds
for Wilhelm, as requested, he certainly brought an eagerness to
talk face to face with his brother and to sit at his own desk and
work on his own research once again. But before that could happen, the count sent him on one last mission to Paris.

Once again Jacob's assignment was to retrieve stolen art treasures. This time he was searching for items taken from neighboring Rhineland, the region between France and Hesse. On this
third trip to France, however, things didn't go quite as well for
Jacob as they had on his previous trips. His job required him to
take paintings and manuscripts away from the same librarians he

had formerly turned to for help when he was doing research in Paris. They did not like losing the materials or being made to look like thieves. "We cannot endure that Monsieur Grimm," said one official, "who comes and works here daily, and yet takes away our manuscripts."

Monsieur Grimm could not endure the French, either. In a letter to Wilhelm, he said that he was "squandering the most beautiful autumn day" on this frustrating work and that he "envied" Wilhelm's "quiet and peaceful" days. When the Second Treaty of Paris was signed on November 20, 1815, Jacob pointed out that it was the second time that the French had tainted their late mother's birthday, the first being during his previous trip with the Hessian delegation. But two weeks later he told Wilhelm that he was finally headed home, "happy that with every step I'm getting nearer to you."

While Jacob was in Paris, Wilhelm was using his "quiet and peaceful" days to put the finishing touches on yet another book — *German Legends*. In some ways these were the tales that didn't quite fit in with *Household Tales*. He and Jacob had decided that these songs and ghost stories, miracle stories and superstitions, were different from fairy tales. A fairy tale, they said, is "more poetic"; a legend is "more historical." A legend was usually connected to a place or a time in history. The story of the Pied Piper of Hameln, for example, was a legend because it is set in a specific city (Hameln is just forty or fifty miles north of Kassel) at a precise moment in history — 1284.

Some of the legends were only a sentence or two long, like the one that told of a statue of Christ in the city of Wittenberg that changed size so that it was always an inch taller than the person standing before it. *German Legends* reads like a Who's Who of mythology. There are water spirits and ghosts, dragons and griffins, werewolves and devils, ghouls and magic garments, dwarves and giants, as well as counts and peasants, soldiers and robbers.

These legends, the brothers believed, were not mere stories. Instead, they "represent the most reassuring and most refreshing of God's gifts to man" because they helped people feel connected to their homes and their country. Ordinary people would forget their history if legends didn't connect it to their lives. Here they could find the stories behind the family names of their princes or the images on their coats of arms. Here they would learn not about some nameless king who behaved nobly or ignobly, but about Prince *Henry* or about Count *Frederick*.

Because these legends, like fairy tales, were rapidly being forgotten, the brothers rescued them, collecting the legends when they encountered them with the kind of surprise, they said, that a child feels when finding a bird's nest in a bush beside the house. "Here, too," wrote Wilhelm in the introduction to this book, "one must quietly lift the leaves and carefully bend back the bough so as not to disturb the folk, if one wishes to steal a furtive glance into the strange yet modest world of nature, nestled into itself, and smelling of fallen leaves, meadow grass, and fresh-fallen rain." *German Legends* was published in 1816 (with a second volume in 1818) but never gained the wide popular appeal the brothers had hoped for.

Since Jacob had resigned from his diplomatic position for Count Wilhelm, he needed a job when he returned from Paris. The director of the library had recently died, and when the deputy director took over that position, it looked as if Wilhelm would be promoted to deputy director. Wilhelm would have liked to move up to his first full-time employment, but working with his brother was even more important to him, so he suggested that Jacob apply for the job.

Wilhelm's selflessness gave the brothers the chance to work together for several years, which were in many ways a wonderfully productive time for both of them. In fact, so that they could continue to work together in Hesse, the region that they so loved, both brothers turned down offers to become professors in a new university that was being started in Bonn, a city to the south of them on the Rhine River. As they worked in the library and in their study, they continued to talk about their work, but they did fewer shared projects.

While Wilhelm kept collecting and revising the fairy tales, Jacob began studying the history of the German language. Jacob seems to have accepted the challenge of August Wilhelm von Schlegel, a famous German writer, who had written that Germany needed a scholar to lay out a history of German language and grammar. Schlegel had also mocked the brothers' high regard for legends and tales, what he called their "respect for every old bit of rubbish."

In taking up the study of grammar, Jacob didn't drop his interest in folktales. Rather, he believed that an understanding of old languages could help explain the development of tales. He discovered that many of the world's languages were related to each other. The Sanskrit spoken in India was related to German just as Latin and Greek were; even English and French were part of the family of languages that came to be called Indo-European. With great

Jacob, as sketched by Ludwig in 1818

excitement he realized that before Sanskrit came to be Sanskrit and German came to be German, people had spoken one language.

Part of the purpose of his *German Grammar* was to explain how languages had changed over the centuries and how they were currently related. These connections were extremely exciting to scholars. In fact, the book sold better than the fairy tales or the legends, becoming something of a national bestseller. Within a year of its publication in 1819, it was sold out, and Jacob began work right away on a second edition.

The work consumed him. He wrote feverishly, staying just a page or two ahead of the printer, who was setting his pages in type and printing them. Even so, the revisions took two years to complete, for it *was* a rather thick book. Jacob explained it—and his excitement—to the Haxthausens:

> *The new edition of my grammar . . . [is] a thick book of one thousand and one hundred pages, horribly printed on poor paper. I will take good care not to send it to you because you would be sure to say, why all this fuss about letters and words! But I will defend myself and answer; the Lord made small things as well as big ones, and everything man looks at closely, is full of wonder: language, word and sound. In a grain of sand we may see the sense and significance of large globes of which our world is one of the smallest.*

One of Jacob's most famous accomplishments was to devise a rule that explained the similarities between words in the Indo-European family. People could see the similarities between, say, the English *father*, the German *Vater*, and the Latin *pater*, but until Jacob's work they could not explain the reason for the similarities. Jacob described the pattern of certain consonant sounds as they changed from the Indo-European language into either Latin or a Germanic language. The pattern could predict when a *p* sound would become an *f* sound or a *b* sound, when a *t* sound would transform into a *th* or a *ð*, when a *k* sound would evolve into a *ch* or a *g*. The rule, which scholars still use today, is known as Grimm's Law, even though Rasmus Rask, a Danish scholar who was working independently around the same time, made the same discovery.

While Jacob was putting the finishing touches on his *Grammar*, Wilhelm was completing the second edition of the fairy tales, which consolidated the two volumes into one. He decided to make *Household Tales* less a book for adults and more a book for children. He didn't want to give in to censors who wanted him to "timidly" cut out "whatever refers to certain situations and relations that take place every day and simply cannot be hidden." By "certain situations and relations" Wilhelm meant sex and pregnancies outside marriage, as well as the kind of violence that Arnim had complained about. He was against cutting those things out of books, he said, because "you can fool yourself into thinking that what can be removed from a book can also be removed from real life." However, he went on, "in this new edition, we have carefully eliminated every phrase not appropriate for children."

Wilhelm *did* remove the stories "How Some Children Played at Slaughtering" and "The Children of Famine," in which a woman wants to eat her children. He also changed the story of Rapunzel to hide the young woman's pregnancy. In the first edition, the witch finds out about the prince's visits when Rapunzel asks why her dresses are now fitting so tightly around her belly. In the second edition, there's no mention of tight dresses, but Wilhelm writes that the two "loved each other dearly, like man and wife." Later on, Wilhelm changed the story even more: the prince asks Rapunzel to marry him as soon as he meets her.

Like any storyteller thinking about his audience, Wilhelm added details to the stories to make them more interesting, becoming more of a reteller and less of a transcriber of the oral tradition. Jacob's first version of "Brier Rose" is quite plain compared with the way that Wilhelm revised it. Jacob had written that "at the moment the King and his court returned, the whole castle fell asleep, everything, even the flies on the walls." Compare that with what Wilhelm wrote:

Sleep extended over the whole palace; the King and the Queen who had just come home, and entered the great hall, began to sleep, and the whole of the court with them. The horses, too, went to sleep in the stable, the dogs in the yard, the pigeons upon the roof, the flies on the wall, even the fire flickering on the hearth became quiet and slept, the roast meat left off frizzling, and the cook, who was just going to pull the hair of the scullery boy, because he had forgotten something, let him go, and went to sleep. And the wind fell, and on the trees before the castle not a leaf moved again.

About the same time, a historical puzzle came to Wilhelm from another direction. Fritz von Schwertzell, an old school friend, had found stones with mysterious marks on them near some ancient burial mounds. The von Schwertzell family asked Wilhelm to try to determine whether the markings were runes, an alphabet used by Germanic and Scandinavian people as early as the year 200, and they promised that he would be the only scholar permitted to examine the stones. True to their word, the family turned away a Professor Dietrich Rommel, who had traveled up from Marburg University on Christmas Eve to examine the stones. Undeterred, Professor Rommel announced to the public that the markings on the stones had been made by humans and that they were probably part of a magic spell, a common use for runes.

Wilhelm looked over the markings and decided that, most

likely, they were not runes. Indeed, scientists later discovered that the "carvings" in the soft rocks had been made by a type of worm. The experience, though, made Wilhelm curious about runes, prompting him to do further research and to write a book, *About German Runes,* which was published in 1821. Professor Rommel, who was later made a nobleman by the count and given a position that Wilhelm had also applied for, was angered by Wilhelm's pronouncements, and his revenge later led to the brothers' departure from their beloved homeland.

In fact, just when the brothers' fame began to spread beyond the German kingdoms, several things happened to let them know that they were not appreciated at home. Because of the many books Jacob and Wilhelm had written, scholars were coming from all over Europe to meet them — so many, in fact, that Jacob grumbled about having to give tours of the palace and its magnificent gardens. By contrast, when Jacob presented the count with the first volume of *German Grammar,* the count said that he hoped Jacob wasn't neglecting his job to work on such "extras."

Shortly after this encounter, Count Wilhelm I died, and his son, Wilhelm II, the prince who had been cheered by the crowds and serenaded by children when he rode into the city after the French occupation, became count. It soon became clear that Wilhelm II's notion of ruling was to oppose whatever his father had done. If his father had required officials to wear pigtails, he would ban them. If his father had supported libraries and the arts, he would not. Jacob and Wilhelm were not so quick to cheer him now. He took away Jacob's funds for buying books and told him that he had to apply to the court chamberlain whenever he wanted money to purchase a specific book. If that weren't enough, the new ruler of Hesse ordered his librarians to make a copy of the library's catalog. The mind-numbing job of writing all the entries by hand took Jacob and Wilhelm a year and a half to complete.

The count's personal life also alienated the brothers and, indeed, many of the people of Hesse. Although he was married, the count moved his mistress, Emilie Ortlöpp, the daughter of a Berlin goldsmith, and her belongings into the palace the day after his father's death. Jacob and Wilhelm felt a strong loyalty to his wife, Countess Augusta, daughter of King Friedrich Wilhelm II of Prussia. In response to the count's behavior, the countess set up a rival court at another castle in Kassel where the Grimms visited to show their loyalty. Wilhelm, in fact, became a history tutor for her son and spent many hours there at dinner with the rival court, listening to music or reading in the evening with the princesses and the ladies-in-waiting. The young prince, son of Countess Augusta and Count Wilhelm II, had "no inner depth" and was "given entirely to superficialities," according to Wilhelm. The young noble was pleasant, but he didn't like studying well enough to suit his tutor.

The brothers' close ties to the countess were risky at a time when the ruler controlled so many aspects of his subjects' lives. Jacob and Wilhelm found this out just before Christmas 1821. During their years as librarians, they hadn't really thought about the fact that they were renting their house from the count. They were suddenly reminded of that fact when they were informed that they would have to move out of their house within two weeks because the count wanted to use the space for offices. The difficulty wasn't only that they would have to give up a house that was just a short walk from the palace and had a beautiful view of its

Countess Augusta

grounds, but also that places to live were hard to find in Kassel. After complaining about the challenge of finding a new house so quickly, the Grimms were given until the following Easter to vacate. Christmas must have been celebrated with mixed emo-tions—thankfulness that they weren't out on the street and sad-ness that they would soon have to leave a home that they had grown to love.

In the spring they found an apartment above a blacksmith shop, hardly the kind of quiet setting that they were accustomed to. Wilhelm, trying to put the best face on the situation, said that he was able to learn a lot of new expressions used by blacksmiths. Yet this turned out to be one of the worst places that the brothers lived. With no view at all, it truly was, as Jacob termed it, "a dark hole."

But if they faced trials during this period, the brothers also found great joy. One such joy was the world's reaction to their fairy tales. In 1823 an Englishman named Edward Taylor translated and published a collection of their fairy tales under the title *German Popular Stories*. Illustrated by the famous English cartoonist George Cruikshank, the book sold tremendously well, enhancing the brothers' reputations even though it didn't put any money in their pockets.

Another great joy was Wilhelm's marriage to Dorothea Wild, the daughter of their old neighbor. Dortchen, as the family called her, had spent the ten years after the death of her father caring for the children of a sister who also had died, but now they were grown. After many years of close friendship with Wilhelm, she was at last free to accept his proposal of marriage. Five years earlier Jacob had included Dortchen's name and birthdate in the family's diary of important dates, so her marriage to Wilhelm was probably not a big surprise to him. And if he was worried about living apart from his brother, he needn't have been, because Wilhelm and Dorothea were quick to invite Jacob to live with them.

Dorothea Wild, ten years before marrying Wilhelm

By now they had found a better place to live, an apartment that overlooked the parks on the other side of Kassel from the count's Wilhelmshöhe. The view from their apartment was of an enormous field surrounding the Orangery, a palace-like greenhouse that rivaled Wilhelmshöhe in the beauty of its ornate exterior. With no houses across from it to disrupt the view, the apartment was a far cry from their rooms above the blacksmith shop. "How beautiful and pure is the smell of the air in the morning and evening," exclaimed Wilhelm in a letter to Jenny von Droste-Hülshoff about their new home, displaying some of the passion for nature that his former companion had found so romantically attractive; "how magnificent the bounteous starry sky and the rising moon!" And best of all, there was room for each brother to have his own study.

The success of Taylor's illustrated English version of the tales

Even in winter, the view of the Orangery and the countryside was beautiful.

The view from Wilhelm's window in 1827

encouraged the Grimms to produce a similar volume for a German audience. Although they had said that they didn't know of any German artist who could compare with the English Cruikshank, they didn't have to look too far to find an artist for the shorter edi-

LEFT: *Ludwig Grimm's illustration of "Brother and Sister"*
RIGHT: *Sketches by Ludwig for the illustration of "Hansel and Gretel"*

tion of *Household Tales*. Their brother Ludwig illustrated the collection of fifty tales, which was published in 1825.

A year later, Dortchen gave birth to her first child. She and Wilhelm named him Jacob. But 1826 turned out to be a sad year for the Grimm family. Late that fall, the baby daughter of Lotte, who had married Ludwig Hassenpflug and was living in Kassel, died, and on the very day of her burial, young Jacob became sick. After several weeks of illness, he, too, died. There was some comfort two years later in 1828 when Dortchen and Wilhelm had a second son, Herman. Yet for a long time after baby Jacob's death, Wilhelm struggled with his sorrow. "At times I grieve more for my loss and have a deeper longing for the child than in the beginning, when I accepted the will of God, and was grateful that he no longer suffered so," he wrote to a friend several years after Jacob had died.

But even as the Grimms adjusted to their loss and pressed on with their lives, more change came. In January 1829, the head librarian died. Jacob applied for his job and Wilhelm applied for Jacob's, both expecting that Wilhelm II would reward their years of good service with these promotions. The count, however, turned down their applications and promoted Wilhelm's old rival, Professor Rommel, instead. In place of the promotions, the count offered the brothers a small raise in pay.

Stung by what they perceived as an insult, they accepted positions at the University of Göttingen in the neighboring province of Hanover.

Wilhelm was to serve as a librarian and Jacob as professor of philology (the study of language and literature) as well as librarian. They handed their resignations to the count. His response shows how little he knew about the fame of the brothers: "So the Grimms are leaving. What a loss!" he said sarcastically. "They have never done anything for me."

Their reputation was repaired somewhat, however, when just before they left Hesse, a foreign ambassador asked the count how he could let such famous scholars leave his service.

Wilhelm, as sketched by Ludwig in 1828

TYPICAL DAY

On a typical day, Wilhelm would be at his desk by 6:30 A.M. for devotions. He would read a passage from the New Testament in Greek, because he thought that the original language was so much purer and simpler than the German translations of the Bible. Around 8:00 A.M. he and Jacob would have coffee together before going to work in the library for three hours between 10:00 A.M. and 1:00 P.M. Both he and Jacob would spend the afternoon working on personal projects like the folktales, usually leaving an hour for a solitary walk, which was so important to each of them.

Professor Rommel was then forced to reveal his role in persuading the count to snub the Grimms, and the count offered Jacob and Wilhelm the positions they had asked for at even higher salaries.

But his offer came too late. Jacob and Wilhelm had given their word to the university, and, even though it was their heart's desire to remain in their homeland, it would not have been honorable for them to break their promise.

After celebrating Christmas 1829 in a virtually empty house, with a tiny tree set on a packing case, Jacob and Wilhelm climbed into a drafty carriage for the cold, day-long trip to Göttingen.

CHAPTER EIGHT

Exile

When the king's daughter saw that there was no hope whatsoever of changing her father's inclinations, she decided to run away. That night, while everyone was asleep, she got up and took three of her precious possessions: a golden ring, a tiny golden spinning wheel, and a little golden reel. She packed the dresses of the sun, the moon, and the stars into a nutshell, put on the coat of all kinds of fur, and blackened her face and hands with soot. Then she commended herself to God and departed. She walked the whole night until she reached a great forest and since she was tired, she climbed into a hollow tree and fell asleep.

—ALL FUR

Although they were older and more experienced now, Jacob and Wilhelm may have felt emotions similar to those they had had when as boys they boarded the carriage to leave Steinau for school in Kassel. Once again they were leaving home and family behind. Dortchen, who was pregnant, wasn't feeling well enough to make the journey, so she and little Herman, now one and a half years old, remained behind as the half-open carriage carried Jacob and Wilhelm off into the biting cold of the December morning. When Dortchen was better, she and Herman would follow.

While Wilhelm carried worries about his wife and child to Göttingen, Jacob carried a little potted houseplant under his coat to their new home. After a cold and lonely carriage ride, they arrived to a warm and welcoming house. A friend who also taught at the university had lit fires in their stoves and set up some of the furniture. And within a couple of weeks Wilhelm returned to Kassel to fetch Dortchen, Herman, and the two maids, who moved with the family. Little Herman made the trip cuddled up with hot water bottles to keep him warm.

Working at the library in Göttingen was not quite as peaceful as working at the library in Kassel. Jacob and Wilhelm could now see that there had been at least one advantage in working for a ruler who didn't really care about books—it gave them the chance to pursue their own interests. Even though they had to spend only six hours a day in the library in Göttingen, they were so busy that they didn't have time to study any of the books. How hard it was for them to be, as Wilhelm said, in the "most famous and most beautiful library in Germany" and not be able to use it the way that they wanted. In addition, their superior, Professor Jeremiah D. Reuss, was strangely secretive about the books he ordered for the library. He wouldn't tell others what he had ordered, and it would often take as much as three years for the books that he did order to appear on the shelves.

Besides the routine library work, there were time-wasting university meetings to attend. Jacob was quick to wonder whether the move had been "a silly thing altogether," although Wilhelm said that he wanted to wait a little before condemning their decision. "At the moment I am still judging," he wrote to Lotte, "but true insight comes only when judging a thing has finished."

Jacob, who was more used to copying ancient texts than he was to teaching, found that it was time-consuming to prepare his lectures in philology. As much as Jacob had admired Professor Savigny's teaching style back when he was a student, he wasn't able to imitate it in his own classroom. Questions and answers would "weaken the teacher's authority," and it was this authority, he thought, that really helped "receptive minds" to learn. It's clear that he was much more interested in being a researcher than a scholar. "Lecturing," he said, "gives me little pleasure and much trouble; I have to consider what the students can use from the material I offer and arrange it and order it for them. I learn nothing from this."

That spring the Grimms moved one more time. They chose a house close to the library and large enough to share with another professor, Otfried Müller. Unlike today's universities in which professors meet students in classrooms, nineteenth-century universities expected the students to go to their professors. Jacob and Müller shared a lecture room on the first floor of the house. Two-year-old Herman Grimm thought this was just great. "Look, there's Apapa!" he would cry, using his special name for Jacob, when he saw his uncle lecturing in the downstairs room.

Just when it began to seem as if life in Göttingen might become routine, if not pleasant, revolution swept across Europe again. Once more the tumult

Jacob "Apapa" Grimm holding nephew Herman

Friends often gathered in the evenings to visit and discuss books.

began in Paris, where in 1830 the people forced King Charles X of France, known for showing favoritism to nobles and for restricting free speech, to give up his throne. The July Revolution, as it came to be called, inspired middle- and lower-class people in neighboring countries to revolt as well. Tired of high taxes and of nobles controlling their lives, citizens called out for representative government and freedom of speech. Throughout the German kingdoms castles were burned and government offices attacked. In Kassel even bakeries were looted.

Universities, then as now, were fertile gardens for new ideas, and student groups eagerly awaited change. Jacob and Wilhelm found themselves torn between the old and the new. They believed in freedom of speech and they knew all too well how kings and counts could abuse their power, but the brothers also knew nobles like Countess Augusta, who, while in exile from her husband and his mistress, had to get soldiers to protect herself from mobs. Then, too, Jacob had seen firsthand the chaos and poverty that followed the French Revolution.

For a time it must have been quite difficult for Jacob and Wilhelm to focus on their books. In January 1831 students rioted in Göttingen. Jacob wrote Professor Savigny that the students wore white armbands and carried swords and rifles as they marched through all the city streets. The conflict lasted around a week until the leaders, several lecturers from the university, were forced by soldiers to flee the region. During the fighting some of the professors were assigned guard duty, and on the last night of the fighting, while he was on watch over the library, Wilhelm came down with a bad case of pneumonia.

For a time it seemed as if Wilhelm might not live. Jacob was distraught and spent many nights at his bedside, caring for his brother and haunted by the fear that Wilhelm would die, leaving him alone in the world. Jacob worried so much that during one of his classes he broke off in mid-lecture and then apologized by saying, "My brother is so sick." What made the time even more difficult for Jacob was news that he felt he had to keep from Wilhelm—that, as he wrote in a letter, "our old true friend Arnim is no more." The person who had helped them publish their first collection of folktales had died just six days before his fiftieth birthday.

The university also was concerned about Wilhelm, both about his health and, if he should die, about his family. Generously, it made him a professor so that Dorothea would have money to support the family in the event of his death. A professor's family received pension money; a librarian's family did not. Both Jacob and Wilhelm remembered how even the small pension that their mother had received had helped after the death of their father, and they were grateful for the protection that this promotion offered Dorothea, Herman, and the youngest child, Rudolph, born three months after they had moved to Göttingen.

After a month and a half of sickness, however, Wilhelm could write his brother-in-law, Ludwig Hassenpflug, that his cough had gotten better "little by little" and that his "outlook was again as it was before the illness." Of course, as Wilhelm recovered, he now was required to lecture as well as work in the library. Jacob worried that the additional work would be hard on Wilhelm, but Wilhelm proved to be more suited to teaching than his brother. He had more patience with his students' mistakes than Jacob did, and he was a very popular lecturer. Twenty-two students signed up for his first class on medieval German poetry (Jacob once had eight for the same class), but Wilhelm thought that many of them had signed up simply because they had to pass an exam in Old High German. He wished that more of them loved learning the way he did, as well as research, which he compared to climbing a mountain path "higher and higher to where the air is pure."

Both brothers expressed their feelings about their work imaginatively. While Wilhelm talked of the joy of breathing the pure air on those ever higher paths, Jacob, according to one of his students, compared himself to an old warrior. Just as the warrior's strength grew in battle, Jacob's grew in his work. The university noticed the increasing national and international honors that Jacob was receiv-

Wilhelm wearing the robes of a university professor

ing. Therefore, to give him more time to do the work he loved the most, the university released him from his library responsibilities and allotted him funds to travel and do research in other regions of Germany. These, however, were still suspicious times, as Jacob found out when officials in Karlsruhe in southern Germany "mutilated" his work by erasing sections of the copies he had made because they might be politically offensive.

Nonetheless, Jacob returned from that trip and another in 1832 with more material for his *Grammar* and more animal tales, like variants of "Reynard the Fox," which he would collect in book form a couple of years later. He also returned with a carefully chosen shawl for Dortchen and a favorite treat of Wilhelm's—ginger nuts—as well as news about the strange new fashions people were wearing: French men were sporting long red trousers and women were wearing very wide skirts (perhaps hoop skirts) that made them look as if they were wearing three or four skirts on top of each other. Dortchen and Wilhelm had news of their own in the summer of 1832—a baby girl. They named her Auguste, after the countess of Hesse, whom they so admired.

More and more honors came their way. Both brothers were made corresponding members of the Academy of Sciences in Berlin, which meant that the most distinguished professors and scientists in the land recognized the importance of their work. In addition, in 1833 Jacob was appointed Privy Councilor to the king of Hanover, an honor, even if the king didn't seek his advice. In an odd twist of history and international marriages, Hanover was now ruled by the king of England, so Jacob was, in effect, councilor to the king of England.

But 1833 was a momentous year for other reasons as well. Hanover approved a new constitution based on the English constitution, granting more rights to the people. The new constitution required all university professors to swear an oath of allegiance to the king. Little did Jacob and Wilhelm know what immense consequences this would have on their lives in just a few years.

Before the test of their character that would thrust them into the national spotlight, they had to face a series of trials of a more private nature. Dortchen and the children visited Lotte, who was ill, in Kassel. While she was sick with the flu and pneumonia, she gave birth to a daughter prematurely. Then Dortchen, who was helping to care for Lotte, got sick as well and came close to dying, according to Wilhelm, who traveled to Kassel to care for his wife and sister.

Dortchen recovered, but Lotte didn't. She took a turn for the worse and died on June 15. Her death was the beginning of a difficult time for both brothers, but particularly for Wilhelm. Over the next two years his own health grew worse. Like many people of his time, he thought that soaking in mineral baths would help to cure him, and so he made two trips to the famous baths at Wiesbaden. The first trip lifted his spirits and made him feel better, but the second wasn't so successful. After that trip, in 1834, his heart problem returned, and he became very depressed.

Jacob and Dortchen didn't know what to do as they watched this normally cheerful man sit moodily all day without working. For almost a year Wilhelm languished, showing little interest in anything. Once again his family was afraid he would die. When he did work, either at home or at the library, he showed no real pleasure in what he was doing. Since Wilhelm wasn't experiencing the joy of climbing "higher and higher" on the trail of ideas, Jacob urged his brother to take an actual vacation, but Wilhelm refused. "Voices demoralize me and make me miserable, unpresentable for social life," Wilhelm wrote to a friend in the summer of 1835, explaining why his "attack of nerves" prevented a visit, "but soon I know that I once more will come with joy [to visit] you." And, indeed, the passage of time did bring healing. Wilhelm gradually returned to writing and in 1836 published a book called *The Rose Garden.*

Jacob, meanwhile, was applying his ideas about fairy tales and the history of language to mythology. His book, *German Mythology,* published in 1835, revolutionized people's thinking, causing one literary historian to say that the subject could be divided into "before Jacob and after Jacob." Before Jacob it was thought that early Germans were crude people with no real culture until the Romans conquered them and passed Roman culture on to them. Jacob argued, however, that "our ancestors lived not in disorderly, untamed hordes, but rather nurtured ancient and traditional, meaningful law . . ." and that "their hearts were full of faith in god and gods, and that happy and grandiose, even if imperfect, ideas of higher beings gave soul and sustenance to their lives."

Yet even as the world applauded Jacob's study of gods and elves and giants, politics disrupted the brothers' lives one more time. In 1837 King William IV—ruler of England, Ireland, and Hanover—died. Queen Victoria took the throne to rule over England and Ireland, but the laws of Hanover forbade a woman to govern the country. Therefore, Victoria's uncle, Ernest Augustus, became king of Hanover in her place. The new king was not kind to Hanover. He revoked the constitution that had been put in place just four years earlier and moved to take away many of the country's freedoms. He also ordered that the professors at the university take an oath of allegiance to him and to his laws.

Many of the professors at Göttingen were outraged at the loss of the constitution, but they were also too afraid of losing their jobs to protest the king's order. "The world," Jacob said, "is full of

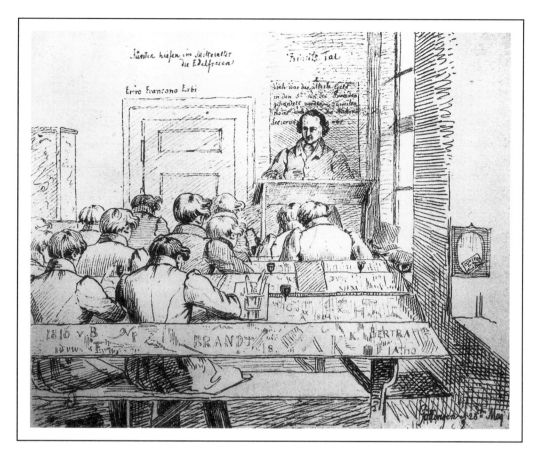

Jacob teaching in Göttingen

men who think and teach what is right. But as soon as they are called upon to act, they are assailed by doubts and fears." He and Wilhelm, however, along with five other professors, stood up to the king. The group, which came to be known as the Göttingen Seven, sent a protest to the king, explaining that they had sworn before God to uphold the constitution and that they could not break an oath made before God.

The protest was quickly noted in Göttingen and throughout Europe. Students demonstrated in the streets, and soldiers were sent to the city to control them. Even though more than fifty students were arrested, others kept up the protest, cheering the

Göttingen Seven and throwing stones through the windows of professors who hadn't stood up to the king. When the students found out that the seven had been fired from the university and that three of the group whom the king perceived as ringleaders—including Jacob—were to be banned from the country, they met at an inn outside the city and voted to take action. They decided to boycott all lectures at the university, send a message of respect to the seven, and let them keep the tuition money that had already been paid (students paid their professors directly). The group also resolved to give the three professors a triumphant send-off.

When the government discovered the students' farewell plan, it quickly imposed a hefty fine—twenty talers—on anyone who provided horses or carriages to students who wanted to accompany the three to the border. Nonetheless, about three hundred students set out to walk the twenty miles through the cold December night. The next day, December 17, 1837, they waited in the town of Witzenhausen, where a bridge crossed the river that served as the border between Hanover and Hesse.

When Jacob and the other professors arrived, accompanied by mounted soldiers, the students unhitched the horses from the professors' coaches and pulled the coaches over the bridge to Hesse. There the students and their heroes gathered at an inn to eat lunch, sing songs, and toast the professors with glasses of wine and mugs of beer. The scene at the bridge became known as the Witzenhausen Escort, and Jacob and the others became minor folk heroes. There was even a metal toy made to depict the scene, with a red-cheeked Jacob lifting his hat to the crowd of students.

Jacob traveled on to stay with his brother Ludwig, who now

was a professor of art in Kassel. Because the rent was paid up for most of the next year, Wilhelm and his family remained in Göttingen until the brothers could decide what to do next. In the coming year he and Jacob would meet several times at a town halfway between Göttingen and Kassel to discuss their options. En route to one such meeting, Jacob and Ludwig stopped at an inn for a meal. There, as they were eating, they overheard two other men talking about the Göttingen Seven and the Witzenhausen Escort. In the midst of the animated conversation, one of the men turned to Jacob and bragged, "I saw Grimm there, with my own eyes!"

While the Göttingen Seven were popular with the people in inns and lecture halls, they were not popular with the nobles who controlled new positions at Germany's universities. Many were afraid of offending the king of Hanover. At moments Jacob and Wilhelm must have felt that perhaps the king was right in his sarcastic remark about their dismissal. "Dancers, whores, and professors could always be got easily for money," he said, and for a time in the beginning of 1838, circumstances appeared to bear him out. No prince or count seemed to value the Brothers Grimm enough to offer them work.

Yet what heartened them was the way they were supported by people who did care about them. Students and faculty at various universities and, indeed, entire towns collected money for the ousted professors. One town, Königsberg, sent 1,600 talers in support of the seven, almost enough in itself to support two professors for a year. When Jacob and Wilhelm balked at taking the money, they were reminded that refusing help would hurt the feelings of those who, like the 130 townspeople of Königsberg, had no other way of showing their support.

But especially touching and sometimes humorous were the neighbors who helped out. The choir director from the Reformed Church in Göttingen tutored Dortchen and Wilhelm's younger son, Rudolph, but refused to charge his normal tuition fees. Then, too, there was the incident with the shopkeeper in Kassel. Ludwig's wife, it seems, had her eye on a certain dress but didn't want to pay twelve talers. When she sent her maid to ask if the wife of Professor Grimm could have it for ten talers, the shopkeeper answered, "Certainly, if it is Frau Professor Grimm from Göttingen. But if it's another, then she must pay twelve."

Although once again their future was uncertain, the brothers had faith that everything would be all right. They could take courage from the confidence that God was caring for them. Wilhelm told a friend that "the greater the tribulation is the more reason to pluck up courage, and leave the inevitable to God. I have often seen that He will find ways we have ourselves not thought of."

CHAPTER NINE

Heroes

Let no one ever say that a poor tailor cannot advance far in the world and achieve great honors. He needs only to hit upon the right person and, most important, to have good luck.

— THE GLASS COFFIN

After leaving Göttingen, Jacob moved once more into the house above the Orangery in Kassel. His brother Ludwig and Ludwig's wife, Marie, now lived there. In the fall of 1838 other tenants moved out of the ground floor, and Jacob was quick to rent it so that Wilhelm's family could come back to Kassel and they could live together once again.

Earlier that summer Jacob had traveled throughout other kingdoms of Germany, even taking the ten-minute trip between the cities of Nuremberg and Fürth on Germany's first railroad. None of the places he visited appeared to be as suitable as Kassel, however, and so when Wilhelm and his family moved in with him in October, the brothers felt as if God were indeed providing for

The market street in Kassel in 1842

them. Yes, they were living in exile, but they were living in the belief that they had done the right thing, and they were living comfortably, for the present time. "As long as there is breath in me," Jacob said, "I will be glad of what I have done." For his part Wilhelm enjoyed working with his brother once again, and he liked living on the ground floor of the house, so that he could simply reach out the window to shake the hands of friends who passed by the house.

While Jacob and Wilhelm were pondering what work they could do next, an offer came from a publisher in the neighboring kingdom of Saxony. Why not work together on a dictionary of the German language? he asked them. Not an ordinary dictionary, but one that would tell how words had been used in the sixteenth, seventeenth, and eighteenth centuries, as well as the nineteenth, a dictionary that would list all words—including obscenities—and quote examples to show how the words were used.

After considering the offer for several months, Jacob and Wilhelm decided to accept it. The project would bring in money that they sorely needed as well as make a contribution to German history. They knew that they could not collect all the words by themselves, so they invited more than fifty other scholars throughout the German kingdoms to help. Jacob and Wilhelm had them take notes on slips of paper that were all exactly the same size so that it would be easier to organize the words as they came in. And come in they did, "settling on our desks like snow on the countryside," said Jacob.

Jacob and Wilhelm enjoyed clearing the "snow" from their desks. The trouble of the recent past made them appreciate this chance to work quietly together. But some of their friends were bothered that the brothers weren't being shown more respect by the universities. One such friend, Bettina von Arnim, the widow of their old friend and herself a writer of some note, pressured the Berlin Academy of Sciences to offer the Grimms positions. She convinced her brother-in-law, their old professor Savigny, to offer them funds for their research. Wilhelm, however, turned down the offer, since the academy could give money only to projects that were assured of success and the dictionary wasn't far enough along to promise success. Wilhelm was also distrustful of the king of Prussia, who had authority over the academy. If the money were to come freely from the professors in the academy, fine — but if it had to be approved by the government, then Wilhelm was wary of it.

Some members of the academy and several of the nobles who were afraid to show support for the notorious Göttingen Seven were offended by Wilhelm's response. Some of them would have liked the brothers to apologize for their protest in Göttingen. The Prussian queen, in particular, spoke against them. She was the sister of the king of Hanover, who had ordered the three Göttingen professors into exile. But the brothers weren't about to step back from their protest. Jacob wrote to Bettina, saying that he thought their protest was very easy to understand:

> *Right and wrong, and the voice of conscience are all that need to be considered. Neither politics nor expediency should come into it; or put it this way: to act according to what is right and listen to the voice of conscience will in the end also be right from the point of view of politics and expediency, and justifiable before God. We did not take into account success. . . .*

Without our protest sheer might would have triumphed, and the whole affair been hushed up.

After all they had been through, the brothers were not going to change their political opinions in order to obtain prestigious positions in Berlin. Fame was not so important to them. Besides, living in Kassel, in a house with a gorgeous view, was not something they were trying to escape.

But in 1840 King Frederick William III of Prussia died, and Jacob and Wilhelm began to think differently about Berlin. The new king, Frederick William IV, was a ruler more to their taste. He not only let many political prisoners out of jail, he also appreciated literature and art.

Now when asked privately by Professor Savigny's wife if he and Wilhelm would go to Berlin, Jacob replied that they wouldn't go just to claim the positions that were rightfully theirs as corresponding members of the academy—but they might go, he suggested, if they were invited more strongly. Their good friend Bettina Arnim did the hinting. She had talked about the Grimms to the king when he was the crown prince, and now she spoke to his advisers about them. Finally, in November 1840 the invitation came. The king, wrote the Prussian Minister of Education, desired that the brothers be given support so that they would have the leisure to work on "the great and very difficult task which you have set yourselves in the completion of a complete critical dictionary of the German language."

For the first time in their lives, Jacob and Wilhelm could be free to work without worrying about money. The king offered them two thousand talers per year to divide as they wished, as well as five hundred talers to pay for their moving expenses. They would have the opportunity to lecture—Jacob immediately and Wilhelm as soon as he was fully inducted into the academy—but they wouldn't have the pressures on their time that they had had in Göttingen. The brothers didn't need to think long about the offer. Jacob slipped into his role as older brother and replied for both of them. We accept, he wrote, with "thankful, joyous faith. Our lives are already on the decline. We strive for nothing during our remaining days but to dedicate ourselves to the completion of our work which covers the language and history of our beloved fatherland. The generosity of the king will furnish us with the worry-free leisure that we need." Jacob added that they would split the money in equal "brotherly" portions.

A few weeks later Jacob made the trip east to Berlin. His arrival there in the middle of the night, he wrote Wilhelm, made for quite "a little adventure." He took a carriage from the post house, but shadows in the moonlight made it nearly impossible to see the house numbers. "After much stumbling about," he found the house of his friend Karl von Meusebach, president of the Court of Appeal, and "began to ring the bell boldly."

But not a soul appeared and no light was visible. This lasted for about a half hour when someone downstairs finally woke up, opened, and at my questioning answered that the Meusebachs did live here. I then went up two flights of stairs to find another locked door where I rang again, but everyone seemed to be fast asleep or deaf. So I sat on the steps until six o'clock, when there was at last a light flickering on the second floor. When I then approached, a man I didn't know

*opened up and simply said that the President's wife seemed to
be home, but that she was alone without servants and that a
cleaning lady would not come until the morning. In the
meantime, he made a friendly invitation to enter his room
where he served me coffee, brought me a newspaper, and kept
me until eight o'clock. When Frau Meusebach awoke,
everything was resolved at once. She had heard no ringing,
and she received me most cordially, took me into my room
that was all ready for me, where I have been sleeping until
now when I report this all to you.*

In a few days, however, Jacob could have wished for a little
less attention. The name Grimm was well known among the artists
and writers of Berlin, and Jacob was invited to many receptions
and dinners. He even had an audience with the king to thank him
for his generous offer. What Jacob had hoped would be a three- or
four-day scouting trip for an apartment soon stretched into several
weeks. It wasn't as easy to find a place to live as he thought it
would be. He looked at more than twenty houses in the icy
December weather, before picking one that Bettina Arnim had suggested. It had been difficult to find something close to the children's
school, and he reported to Wilhelm and Dortchen that the children
would have a twenty-minute walk. But, Jacob said, they could take
a cab in bad weather and, with its balcony and ten rooms, the
"quiet, open and cheerful" apartment was just right for them. Best
of all, the apartment looked out over the Tiergarten, an enormous
park that could help the Grimms forget that they were in the big
city. His business finally completed, Jacob headed back to Kassel
on the day before Christmas.

In February 1841 the brothers began the bittersweet process of packing up for their move to Prussia. It was hard, Wilhelm said, to choose what to take and what to leave behind. It was hard, too, to leave the region that they loved so well, even though they hadn't been fully recognized by their fellow Hessians. Making the move even more difficult, both Jacob and Dortchen became sick. Jacob complained of pressure in his chest and didn't leave his room for three weeks, and Dortchen spent a week in bed. Everyone was well enough by March to make the trip to Berlin, but upon their arrival with two enormous cartloads of books and other possessions, they discovered that the house wasn't ready. They spent a week at an inn and then lived for weeks among their boxes because Dortchen still wasn't healthy enough to set up their household things.

Living in Berlin took some getting used to. Although the area in which they lived was quiet, the constant sound of carriage wheels disturbed Wilhelm, and, he wrote a friend, the sight of the long streets "with no visible end to them makes me tired from the outset." To get away from the noise and the busyness of the city, he and Jacob regularly took walks through the park across the street, enjoying its "stately trees" and flowers and its pools with "thousands of goldfish" and finding solitude on paths that few other Berliners used.

Their popularity also took some getting used to. Both brothers were met with loud cheers when they gave their first public lectures as members of the academy in the spring of 1841. Instead of the handful of students that they had grown accustomed to in Göttingen, audiences of several hundred turned out. It was an emotional experience for each of the brothers. Jacob's voice trem-

Potsdam Palace in 1857

bled, and he had to stop several times to collect himself, and Wilhelm's eyes filled with tears at the cheering of the students. Although they were not required to do so, both Jacob and Wilhelm gave numerous public lectures over the next few years, although Jacob felt much less comfortable speaking in public than did Wilhelm.

There were also numerous social events to attend. The Grimms dined with princes and with the king. They were added to the list of celebrities who were invited to attend royal performances at the new palace in Potsdam, just outside Berlin. Jacob and Wilhelm joined the others on a special train that took them to Potsdam to see the performances. On one occasion they were invited not to the concert but to a large, fancy dinner party instead. When they arrived, however, they discovered that all of the other dinner guests had been commanded to attend the king's concert, so the Grimms and their host had the fricassée of pike, truffle pastries, and orange sorbet all to themselves.

Birthdays had always been important to Jacob and Wilhelm, and in Berlin they discovered that they had to work to keep them small family celebrations. Students and other admirers would gather around their house, sometimes with torches, calling for Jacob and Wilhelm to appear on the balcony. When the brothers came out, the crowd would sing songs and deliver speeches and gifts to them.

One such celebration turned out unhappily for the brothers. In 1844 August Hoffmann, a writer and professor who had been exiled by the king from Breslau, a city in present-day Poland, was invited to Wilhelm's birthday party. The Grimms told him that students were planning a torchlight celebration. When the students arrived, they recognized Hoffmann, and he spoke to them in the street. What the Grimms didn't know was that Hoffmann had gotten in trouble for writing political poems and was being watched by the police, who judged his talk to the birthday crowd to be an anti-government demonstration. As a result, he was expelled from Berlin—and the Grimms were attacked in the newspapers for refusing to defend him. They, on the other hand, believed that Hoffmann had played a "mean, inconsiderate trick" on them, abusing their hospitality in order to upset

Bettina Arnim

the king. They believed Hoffmann knew that the king would think that they, the Brothers Grimm, whose salaries he paid, had supported a public demonstration for a dismissed professor. As it turned out, the king understood the Grimms' position, and most other people believed that the brothers had acted with integrity, just as they had in Göttingen.

Perhaps the hardest part of the controversy for Jacob and Wilhelm was the fact that their longtime friend Bettina Arnim spoke out against them. Some people even believe that she helped to set up the pro-Hoffmann demonstration. The incident destroyed their friendship for almost fifteen years, until Wilhelm's son Herman married Bettina's daughter, Gisela.

The newspapers and the public forgot the incident rather quickly, however, particularly in light of the many honors that were being conferred on Jacob and Wilhelm from all over the world. Prussia granted Jacob its highest award, the *Pour le mérit,* the first time it had been given to someone not in the military. France gave Jacob the Cross of the Legion of Honor. England made Jacob and Wilhelm members of the Philological Society, a group of scholars who studied language, and the United States admitted Jacob as a foreign member of the Academy of Arts and Sciences.

Scholars and admirers came from all over Europe to visit the famous brothers. Although Jacob and Wilhelm hated the interruption of their work, they were usually cordial to visitors, inviting them to tea or taking them on walks in the gardens across from their house. Not surprisingly, however, the visits could be a bit awkward, particularly if the less socially adept Jacob was the only one at home. The famous Danish storyteller Hans Christian

Andersen wrote in his autobiography, *The Story of My Life*, about the embarrassment he felt when, on his first visit to Berlin, Jacob didn't know who he was:

> *I had not brought any letters of introduction to them with me, because people had told me, and I myself believed it, that if I were known to anybody in Berlin, it must be the brothers Grimm. I therefore sought out their residence. The servant-maid asked me with which of the brothers I wished to speak. "With the one who has written the most," said I, because I did not know, at that time, which of them had most interested himself in the "Märchen."*
>
> *"Jacob is the most learned," said the maid-servant.*
>
> *"Well, then, take me to him."*
>
> *I entered the room, and Jacob Grimm, with his knowing and strongly marked countenance, stood before me.*
>
> *"I come to you," said I, "without letters of introduction, because I hope that my name is not wholly unknown to you."*
>
> *"Who are you?" asked he.*
>
> *I told him, and Jacob Grimm said, in a half-embarrassed voice, "I do not remember to have heard this name. What have you written?"*
>
> *It was now my turn to be embarrassed in a high degree, but I mentioned my little stories.*
>
> *"I do not know them," said he, "but mention to me some other of your writings, because I certainly must have heard them spoken of."*
>
> *I named the titles of several, but he shook his head. I felt myself quite unlucky.*

"But what must you think of me," said I, "that I come to you as a total stranger, and enumerate myself what I have written: You must know me! There has been published in Denmark a collection of the "Märchen" of all nations, which is dedicated to you, and in it there is at least one story of mine."

"No," said he good-humoredly, but as much embarrassed as myself. "I have not read even that, but it delights me to make your acquaintance. Allow me to conduct you to my brother Wilhelm?"

"No, I thank you," said I, only wishing now to get away. I had fared badly enough with one brother. I pressed his hand and hurried from the house.

When Wilhelm found out about the visit, he explained to Jacob who Andersen was, and in later years Andersen and the Grimms exchanged visits and stories.

Visitors would sometimes note that it was hard to keep up with Jacob on their walks because he was so eager to get back to the house to write. Indeed, with their busy social life in Berlin, it is amazing that Jacob and Wilhelm got any writing done, but somehow they did. They kept at the dictionary which, they soon realized, was a much bigger task than they had thought at the outset, and they also edited a fifth edition of *Household Tales*, which was published in 1843. Taking breaks from working on the dictionary, which wasn't his first love, Wilhelm published two books on medieval legends in the 1840s. And as much as he believed in the dictionary, Jacob decided that people needed a history of the German language more.

In some ways, the *History of the German Language* was the story

Wilhelm and Jacob in an etching by Ludwig in 1843

behind the piles of notes that covered Jacob's and Wilhelm's desks. As he looked at the many slips of paper (at one point, there were more than 600,000 of them), Jacob saw how words had changed as people had changed. In 1847 he was able to quickly write the book, which appeared the following year in two volumes. In it he showed how history altered the language that people used, how wars with the Romans or the French altered words as well as treaties.

But even as he was finishing the book, Jacob could hear gunfire from the streets. Another revolution was making history.

CHAPTER TEN

From A to ?

From then on they lived happily, and everything went well for them until they died.

—THE GOLDEN CHILDREN

In 1848 events once more pulled Jacob into politics. Again, the revolution began in France, where people took to the streets to overthrow their king. Throughout Europe, there was a hunger for the kind of freedom that came with constitutions. People were tired of kings and princes who cared more about their own power and privilege than about their subjects' health and happiness. And so the revolution quickly spread. Nationalist leaders in Hungary called for a constitution. Fighting broke out in Italy. Skirmishes in Vienna made the Austrian ruler flee the country. The Bavarian king stepped down. Leaders in several German kingdoms spoke out for a constitution that would unify the German states just as the United States constitution had unified the American states;

Hesse and Bavaria, Hanover and Prussia, would be like Maine and Massachusetts, Georgia and New York.

King Frederick William of Prussia had consistently refused to consider a constitution. When he saw how bad the conflict in Austria was, he announced some changes: he would abolish censorship and open the door to a constitution. But he had already ordered large numbers of soldiers to Berlin. On March 18, 1848, the same day that he changed his mind, his soldiers fired on people gathered around the palace. Wilhelm wrote to Ludwig that at two o'clock everyone was celebrating, and at three o'clock people were being shot. "For a full fourteen hours," wrote Wilhelm, "twenty to twenty-five thousand soldiers fought fiercely against the people in the streets. The clattering volleys from rifles and the booming of cannons and shells were quite horrible, especially at night." At least 230 civilians were killed in the fighting, but the troops were still not able to clear the barricades that the people had erected.

When he saw the devastation to his capital and his people, the king ordered the troops out of Berlin and took part in a ceremony in which he handed over arms to the citizens' militia. Wearing the red, black, and gold that stood for a Germany of united kingdoms, the king said, "I wear colors which are not mine . . . I do not want a throne, I do not want to rule. I want Germany's freedom, Germany's unity." Later that day he said, "Henceforth, Prussia merges into Germany." People weren't exactly certain what that would mean, but they were happy that it opened the way for elections for a Prussian state congress and for a parliament to discuss the unification of the German kingdoms.

Representatives from all the German kingdoms were chosen for the parliament in Frankfurt, and in May 1848 Jacob was one of the 350 who began discussing the fate of Germany. Newspapers praised him for "his stern character" and his courage as a member of the Göttingen Seven. Like Jacob, many of the representatives to the Frankfurt parliament were professors—and it showed in their discussions. They were better at debating abstract ideas than they were at taking the practical steps to set up a government.

Yet set up a government they did, picking the officials to rule and asking other countries to recognize the new Germany. While Sweden, the Netherlands, the United States, and some other smaller countries accepted the new government, the powerful countries in Europe found it hard to take the new Germany seriously. It had no real power, no money, no constitution, and a parliament that seemed to like discussion better than action. When the new minister of the army ordered parades as a way of marking the establishment of the new government, many of the states refused. The government in Hanover, for example, said that the weather wasn't good enough for a parade.

By August 1848 Jacob had had enough of quarrels about politics, and he resigned from the parliament. The government eventually fell apart. It would be more than twenty years before there was a unified Germany. But Jacob's participation in the Frankfurt parliament and his enthusiasm for a German nation colored his *History of the German Language.* The Germans, he wrote, were a great race of people who, by overturning the Roman Empire, brought freedom to other European countries. He also suggested that Denmark, which was in a border dispute with Prussia at the time, would be taken over by a unified Germany. There are two types of peoples, he continued, those who are great and capable of ruling and those who are submissive and conquered. Those who are great "seem as if they finally will master the world." Unfortunately, it was this type of patriotism that, ninety years later, helped to justify the destruction of non-Germans by the Nazis. The Nazis loved the Germanic emphasis here and elsewhere in the brothers' work, and Hitler's propaganda office distorted Jacob and Wilhelm's literary patriotism to support their own program of racism.

Jacob returned from Frankfurt eager to pick up his work on the dictionary. It wasn't long before he could say that he was "engrossed, almost buried" in the project. He was working on *A* through *C*, and Wilhelm was working on *D*. When by 1854 they were able to publish only the first volume, *A–Biermolke*, Jacob realized that he wouldn't be able to finish the dictionary in his lifetime. In fact, it wasn't completely finished for one hundred years.

With the end of the work nowhere in sight, Jacob had second thoughts about having asked Wilhelm to work with him. "In my heart," Jacob wrote a friend, "I have often reproached myself for having driven him into matters of grammar which are contrary to his inclination." Wilhelm was quite often depressed, and, at least from Jacob's perspective, the brothers didn't work together as well now as they had on the fairy tales. Part of the problem may have been that Wilhelm wouldn't do things the way that Jacob wanted him to. Their studies were next door to each other, and Jacob complained that Wilhelm took books into his room and left them on tables, where they were hard for Jacob to find when he wanted them. And if Wilhelm *did* bring the books back, there was the annoying noise of the "ceaseless" opening and closing of doors. But even worse, complained Jacob, was the fact that Wilhelm "feels quite independent and is slow to agree where opinions dif-

Wilhelm's study in Berlin

Jacob's study in Berlin

fer." In this letter Jacob comes off as rather grumpy and hard to please. It's obvious that what Jacob wanted was a clone of himself.

Even though they lived and worked together and shared some similar habits, Jacob and Wilhelm had distinctive personalities. Visitors who came to see the Brothers Grimm often noted the differences. A writer named Julius Rodenberg, for example, saw Wilhelm as a less intimidating figure than Jacob. When he first met the brothers, Rodenberg found Wilhelm to be "a man with a quietly contented face" and "blue eyes and long grey hair," looking more like "a man of feeling than an intellectual." Wilhelm didn't "intimidate through intellectual superiority," said Rodenberg.

Jacob, on the other hand, was "quite different" on first impression. The older Grimm, Rodenberg said, "inspires a little nervousness" because of his intense eyes and hasty manners. With a little more time and conversation, Jacob seemed less intimidating, but he was often awkward socially. He could be abrupt in letters and in conversation, ignoring social niceties in order to make a point. Few things made him as happy as his research. He was pleased when the weather was bad and he could skip his walk in the park, working at his desk from early morning until late at night. Still, even the serious scholar had his playful side. Wilhelm's daughter, Auguste, recalls preparing for a vacation to the Harz Mountains . . . and seeing her uncle sitting at the dining room table wearing her mother's straw hat with ribbons over his long white hair.

Rules of etiquette were not Jacob's forte. Once at a birthday luncheon for the king, Jacob came close to making a social blunder that could have insulted the ruler. Since the party hosted by the Grimms' old friend Savigny was formal, Dortchen had sewn

Jacob's medals on his coat. At the meal Jacob sat passing the lavish dishes of food, listening to the tinkling sound of his medals, and wondering what he could say to make conversation. Then, when Savigny proposed a toast to the king, Jacob knew. He would rise and say a few words about Savigny's latest book on Roman law. Seeing Jacob about to stand up, his neighbor at the table told him that he could do what he wanted but it wasn't proper to toast another person after the royal toast had been given. Jacob felt angry; he couldn't see how it would harm the king to honor someone so obviously deserving as Savigny. But he lost his train of thought and reluctantly remained quiet.

In the fall of 1859 Wilhelm and Dortchen and the children took a rare vacation trip on the nearby Elbe River. A few years before, they had managed a vacation on the Rhine, but generally Wilhelm's health kept the family close to home, while Jacob occasionally traveled to places more remote like Austria, Sweden, and even Italy. But in December, not long after Wilhelm and Dortchen returned from their small trip, he became sick. He had some kind of infection that produced a fever as well as a small bump on his back, called a carbuncle, where the skin was infected. Doctors drained the carbuncle, but it resisted healing.

Dortchen and Jacob were worried about Wilhelm, but then were relieved when he felt better. When he sat up in bed one day, Wilhelm said what others were thinking: "God be praised! I had really thought it would end fatally, and I have still so much to do." Resting in bed, Wilhelm looked over page proofs for a new book and set aside gift copies of the latest edition of the fairy tales for friends. But on the night of December 15 the fever came back. At one time in the night while he was delirious, Wilhelm looked up at Jacob and recognized him but thought he was a painting. "It looks very like him," said Wilhelm. Eventually, he slept, and Jacob thought he was doing better. Near dawn, Jacob heard Wilhelm breathing quietly and believed that the worst was over. "Ah, my God!" Jacob said later. "I had thought all would now go on well."

For a time on the sixteenth Wilhelm seemed at least to be thinking clearly. One of Wilhelm's children wrote that it was "unspeakably moving to see Apapa sitting," leaning close to his brother to hear whatever he might say. Wilhelm talked about a lot of different things, first politics, then scholarship, then about things in general during a happy but measured conversation. In fact, just "two hours before his death he told one of his favorite stories in an eastern dialect and laughed at himself about it." But then, at three o'clock in the afternoon, Wilhelm died.

His body was laid out in his study. As he lay surrounded by the work and memorabilia of his life, Jacob frequently came in to look long and earnestly at the friend and brother he would not see again.

People in Berlin had gotten so used to thinking of the Brothers Grimm together that they thought Jacob must be going berserk without Wilhelm. The newspapers wrote articles claiming that Jacob was roaming the empty rooms of the house in despair, looking for Wilhelm. The truth, according to Wilhelm's son Herman was nothing like this. Jacob was sad, but "there was no change perceptible in his general demeanor." Jacob did his "customary work," but it was with a great sense of loss that he moved his brother's notes and books into his own study to resume working on them. He saw to the publication of the last book that Wilhelm had been writing, a translation of a book on moderation by a medieval writer. Ironically, given the subject, Jacob had the book bound in the most expensive covers possible.

There was, of course, still the dictionary to occupy his mind, and Jacob turned to the job with great discipline. Wilhelm had finished work on the letter *D,* and by 1860 Jacob was able to send a second volume to be printed. Still, as Jacob explained to the publisher, reminders of Wilhelm were everywhere: "I cannot get rid of my sad thoughts; I wish I were able to get back to my old ways of working." Every time Jacob passed the study next to his, the room spoke to him of Wilhelm. Except for the papers and books that Jacob was using for the dictionary, Wilhelm's things in his study had been left untouched; arrangements had been made for an artist to paint a picture of the room.

Although regular walks in the Tiergarten helped keep Jacob healthy, he had a harder and harder time sleeping at night. He would awaken in the middle of the night and think about his life. Sometimes he would write down his thoughts on little cards and put them in his pocket. In June 1862 he made this note and tucked it away:

> *How beautiful the long summer days, hailed with joy by birds and men! They recall the springtime of life, when the hours drink in the light and flow slowly away; what remains is swallowed up in the gloom of winter and old age. Now I shall soon be seventy-eight; and when I lie sleepless in bed the dear, soft light comforts me, and inspires thoughts and memories.*

Since his childhood Jacob had loved looking at the stars and picking out favorite constellations, like the Pleiades, and now when he couldn't sleep he would go to the window and gaze at the great array of stars.

In the spring of 1863 Jacob's younger brother Ludwig, the artist, died. "Now I am the only one left," said Jacob. As part of his research for an essay on old age, Jacob read a book on longevity that suggested that people could live to be a hundred years old. He joked that that was what he planned to do, but in at least one part of his mind he was thinking about dying. Shortly after Wilhelm's death, he said that he would "follow after this beloved brother before long," to be "close by him forever" in death as he "always was in life."

Early that fall Jacob took a little trip, and while the vacation in the Harz Mountains seemed to do him good, he caught a cold shortly after he got back home. The cold led to what the doctors called inflammation of the liver, which seemed to get better after the doctor put leeches on him and gave him a mercury-based medicine. Although the medicine was sometimes used as a poison, Jacob started doing quite well, at least during the daytime. He was strong enough to sit up in bed and read for hours at a time. Nighttime, however, was a different story. He was "restless and feverish," Herman reported. The doctor thought that Jacob might sleep better at night if he would get out of bed during the day, so the family gave it a try.

On a Saturday afternoon in September, the family got Jacob up for the second time. He sat in his usual wicker chair near the window next to the thirty-one-year-old Auguste. When her uncle suddenly leaned against her and then didn't answer a question she asked him, Auguste was frightened. She thought that Jacob was dead or that he had fainted.

Jacob wasn't dead, but he had suffered a stroke in the part of his brain that controlled the right side of his body. His tongue and his arm were paralyzed, and he couldn't speak. He touched his right arm with his left, as if, thought Herman, he wanted to discover what was wrong with it. Jacob stayed much the same through the night on Saturday and through the day on Sunday. At times, said Auguste, his heart beat so wildly she thought it would explode, and once, said Herman, "we thought we had lost him, when suddenly he took up a photograph of Wilhelm, brought it close before his eyes, as he was wont to do, looked at it for some moments, and laid it down upon the coverlet." Finally, just past ten o'clock at night on September 20, 1863, Jacob looked steadily for a moment at the family gathered around him and then, in Auguste's words, "set his eyes toward his new eternal home."

Afterword

A great many people turned out for Jacob's funeral in September 1863, and newspapers as well as scholarly journals published articles of appreciation. Future generations would argue about which of Jacob and Wilhelm's contributions were the most valuable. Some would say that Grimm's Law and the history of language were most important. Others would argue for the dictionary. But most people would remember the Brothers Grimm for the fairy tales. As they intended, they preserved the tales for German readers, but they also gave them to the world. The tales would be translated into more than 160 different languages, from Afrikaans and Azerbaijani to Vietnamese and Yiddish, in thousands of different editions. The list of artists who illustrated the tales reads like a Who's Who of children's book illustration: George Cruikshank, Walter Crane, Arthur Rackham, Kay Nielsen, W. W. Denslow, Johnny Gruelle, Wanda Gág, Maurice Sendak, Arnold Lobel, Trina Schart Hyman, James Marshall, Paul Zelinsky, and many, many others. Movie studios adapted many of the stories over the years. But whatever we might remember about the work of the Brothers Grimm, we must also remember them for the lives that produced that work, lives of discipline and faith, of love and integrity, lives lived simply and well.

Publications of the Brothers Grimm

Both individually and as a team, Jacob and Wilhelm Grimm published hundreds of items in periodicals and books. Some were scholarly essays or reviews of books, but many were versions of poems, songs, or stories that the brothers had found elsewhere. In publishing them, the Grimms and their generation of scholars were applying the latest technology to the literature of the Middle Ages.

Just as people today put books and reference materials in digital formats that can be searched and read on computers, nineteenth-century scholars placed information from hand-copied manuscripts into printed books that could be widely distributed. The printing press had been invented around 1450, and books were readily available to middle-class families like the Grimms. Many of the oldest stories, however, were still in manuscript form, found only in the libraries of monasteries, the nobility, and individual countries.

BOOKS PUBLISHED JOINTLY BY THE BROTHERS GRIMM

Die beiden ältesten deutschen Gedichte aus dem achten Jahrhundert: Das Lied von Hildebrand und Hadubrand und das Weissenbrunner Gebet (The Two Oldest German Poems of the Eighth Century: The Song of Hildebrand and Hadubrand and the Wessobrunn Prayer), 1812. Written down around 825, the first poem tells the tragic story of Hildebrand, who is forced to fight his own son, Hadubrand, in battle. It is the only surviving example of the heroic songs that were sung at the courts of Germanic kings. The second, an earlier poem written between 787 and 815, is a prayer that asks the God of creation to protect the speaker of the prayer.

Kinder- und Hausmärchen (Children's and Household Tales), vol. I, 1812; vol. II, 1815; second edition (2 vols.), 1819; vol. III, 1822; third edition (2 vols.), 1837; fourth edition (2 vols.), 1840; fifth edition (2 vols.), 1843; sixth edition (2 vols.), 1850; seventh edition (2 vols.), 1857. Volume I contained 86 tales and volume II 70, some of them fragments or multiple versions of the same tale. In the later editions, which they described as *vermehrte und verbesserte* (enlarged and improved), the brothers removed 32 tales but added others until they reached the 210 of the seventh edition. They also published a one-volume *kleine Ausgabe* (shorter edition) in 1825, which contained 50 tales as well as several illustrations by their brother Ludwig Emil. The third volume, revised by Wilhelm in 1856, provided notes and discussed the particular histories of the tales.

Altdeutsche Wälder (Old German Miscellany), vol. I, 1813; vol. II, 1815; vol. III, 1816. The Grimms published almost forty articles in this periodical, which they edited. They wrote about Norse heroic songs and Germanic legends, but they also introduced folk literature from Holland, France, Serbia, India, and other countries.

Der Arme Heinrich von Hartmann von der Aue (The Poor Heinrich of Hartmann von der Aue), 1815. The Grimms used old manuscripts from the Vatican and from Strassburg to produce a new version and commentary of this old German poem written by a twelfth-century minstrel and crusader. Even though they were poor at the time, the brothers donated the proceeds from the book's sale to rebuilding Hesse after Napoleon's occupation.

Lieder der Alten Edda (Songs of the Elder Edda), vol. I, 1815. No other volumes were published. Working from a manuscript, the brothers edited and commented on this, the oldest Icelandic poem.

Deutsche Sagen (German Legends), part I, 1816; part II, 1818. Unlike fairy tales, as the brothers explained in their introduction to these two volumes, legends have some connection to real people or to historical places and events.

Irischen Elfenmärchen (Fairy Legends and Traditions of the South of Ireland), ed. Thomas Croften Croker, trans. from the English by the Brothers Grimm, 1826. The Grimms included twenty-seven out of the thirty-eight tales that Croker had collected as a child, and the introduction that they wrote for this German edition was translated into English for later editions of the original book.

Deutsche Wörterbuch (German Dictionary), vol. I, *A–Biermolke*, 1854. Although the brothers began planning it in 1838, the dictionary would not be completed until a hundred years after Jacob's death. It took so long because it was designed to describe the ways that people used words, not to prescribe the ways that they ought to use them. The brothers collected sentences from books showing the meaning of each word as it had been written by an earlier author.

BOOKS BY JACOB GRIMM

Über den altdeutschen Meistergesang (On Old German Master Song), 1811. Jacob argued that, contrary to current opinion, the fourteenth-century singers, who were often craftsmen (like shoemakers or carpenters), used the same kind of poetry as the Minnesingers who sang songs of love and chivalry in the aristocratic courts of the twelfth and thirteenth centuries.

Besinnungen aus meinem Leben (Reflections on My Life), 1814. The fact that Jacob was only twenty-nine when he wrote this autobiography wasn't unusual for the time period. Life expectancy was considerably shorter then than it is today, and Jacob already had lived through a number of notable events.

Silva de Romances viejos (Old Spanish Heroic Poems), 1815. Jacob did not translate these poems when he published them because he believed that any educated person ought to be able to read Spanish.

Irmenstrasse und Irmensäule: Eine mythologische Abhandlung von Jacob Grimm. (Irmenstrasse und Irmensäule: A Mythological Discussion by Jacob Grimm), 1815. Drawing on myths from around the world and on some of the folklore collected in *Old German Miscellany,* Jacob discussed patterns he observed.

Deutsche Grammatik (German Grammar), vol. I , 1819; vol. II, 1826; vol. III, 1831. In his description of the German language, Jacob not only defined the principle that has come to be known as Grimm's Law but also coined the terms "Old High German" and "Middle High German" to describe different historical dialects of German. These terms are still commonly used today.

Wuk's Stephanowitsch [Karadzic] kleine Serbische Grammatik verdeutscht und mit einer Vorrede von Jacob Grimm: Nebst Bermerkungen über die neuste Auffassung langer Heldenlieder aus dem Munde des Serbischen Volks, und der Übersicht des merkwürdigsten jener Lieder von Johann Severin Vater (Vuk Stefanovic Karadzic's Small Serbian Grammar Translated into German by and with a Foreword by Jacob Grimm: Including Remarks About the Newest Interpretation of Serbian Oral Epic Heroic Folk Songs and the Summary of the Most Remarkable Features of Each Song by Johann Severin Vater), 1824. This project is in part a result of Jacob's apparent boredom during the eight months he spent at the Congress of Vienna. To give himself something to do, he "became acquainted" with Slavic languages, learning Czech well enough to read Czech folktales and becoming fluent enough in Serbian to translate this grammar.

Deutsche Rechtsaltertümer (German Legal Antiquities), 1828. In this project, Jacob was drawing on his legal training and working to demonstrate the value of German culture in an area where it had been overlooked by scholars.

Reinhart Fuchs (Reynard the Fox), 1834. Jacob had been comparing versions of this old trickster tale since his first trip to Paris in 1804.

Deutsche Mythologie (German Mythology), 1835. Jacob wanted this study of Germanic myths to change ideas about German culture, hoping it would dispel the misconception that the ancestors of Germans were wild, disorderly, uncultured hordes. Since so much of the book is still considered an important source of information on German myth, Jacob achieved his goal.

Über seine Entlassung (Concerning My Dismissal), 1838. This is Jacob's explanation of his involvement with the Göttingen Seven and his banishment from the university and the province of Hanover.

Lateinische Gedichte des X. u. XI. Jahrhunderts (Latin Poems of the Tenth and Eleventh Centuries), 1838. Even though these poems were in Latin, they were all written in Germany by German writers.

Weistümer (Legal Precedents), vols. I and II, 1840; vol. III, 1842; vol. IV, 1863; vol. V, 1866; vol. VI, 1869. Presenting a survey of old legal practices and common law, this series of volumes came to be a valuable source book of German legal history.

Geschichte der deutschen Sprache (History of the German Language), 2 vols., 1848. Research on the German dictionary convinced Jacob of the need for a history of the German language. However, because he wrote it during the revolution of 1848, the history is unfortunately colored with excessively patriotic arguments.

BOOKS BY WILHELM GRIMM

Altdänische Heldenlieder, Balladen und Märchen (Old Danish Heroic Songs, Ballads, and Fairy Tales), trans. into German by Wilhelm Grimm, 1811. Some of these Danish songs of chivalry were very old—older even than the Germanic poem the "Nibelungenlied," which Wilhelm was studying when he first came across some of these poems.

Drei altschottische Lieder in Original und Übersetzung aus zwei neuen Sammlungen (Three Old Scottish Songs in the Original Language and Translated out of Two New Compilations), 1813. Never narrow in his interests, Wilhelm, like his brother, collected tales and songs from all over Europe, including these from Scotland.

Über deutsche Runen (About German Runes), 1821. This study of the ancient alphabet was occasioned when a friend asked Wilhelm to investigate the markings on rocks discovered on the friend's estate.

Zur Literatur der Runen: Nebst Mittheilung runischer Alphabete und gothischer Fragmente aus Handschriften (On the Literature of the Runes: Together with Information on a Runic Alphabet and Gothic Fragment in Manuscript Form), 1828. A book that grew out of Wilhelm's earlier investigation of the carvings on rocks, this was the first substantial exploration of the ancient markings on artifacts like helmets and religious tablets.

Grâve Ruodolf (Count Rudolf), 1828. Although some of this medieval poem about the Crusades was missing, Wilhelm patched together the fragments he could find and published as complete an edition as possible.

Die deutsche Heldensage (German Heroic Tales), 1829. Jacob later spoke of this retelling of the tales that dated from the sixth to the sixteenth century as Wilhelm's greatest achievement. According to Wilhelm, before this collection preserved them, some of these stories were known by as few as twelve people.

De Hildebrando antiquissimi carminis teutonici fragmentum edidit Guilelmus Grimm (The Song of Hildebrand Edited by Wilhelm Grimm from an Old Germanic Fragment), 1830. Working from a Latin version of the same poem that he and Jacob had edited as their first book together, Wilhelm produced a more complete version of the heroic tale.

Vridankes Bescheidenheit (The Wisdom of Freidank), 1834. Wilhelm reconstructed this medieval text on morality from several fragments in manuscript form. Freidank was a medieval writer who had participated in the Fifth Crusade in 1228. He wrote many brief poems setting forth his reflections on life.

Der Rosengarten (The Rose Garden), 1836. In this medieval poem, which is very much like the legend of King Arthur except for the German names of the characters, King Dietrich of the Goths fights with the warrior Siegfried.

Ruolandes liet (The Song of Roland), 1838. This edition presents the first complete text in German of the French heroic poem about Charlemagne's nephew, who was killed in a battle against the Saracens in 778.

Wernher von Niedderrhein (Werner from Lower Rhineland), 1839. Named for the priest who wrote it, this medieval poem attempted to explain the words of Jesus by using very symbolic language.

Konrads von Würzburg Goldene Schmiede (Konrad of Würzburg's Golden Smithies), 1840. Wilhelm was the first to publish this thirteenth-century poem about the Virgin Mary.

Konrads von Würzburg Silvester (Konrad of Würzburg's Silvester), 1841. This thirteenth-century poem tells the story of the first pope of the Roman Empire as he does such things as saving Rome from a dragon, curing Constantine of leprosy, and resurrecting a bull that had been killed.

Über Freidank (On Freidank), 1855. Wilhelm was very interested in this writer who condemned arrogance, greediness, and envy and who warned against getting too attached to the things of the world. Those who serve God, according to Freidank, have found the direction of wisdom.

A Few Words About Sources

I've tried to ensure that all of the information in this book is accurate. I did not make up scenes or conversation. When I write that a room had green wallpaper or that the brothers ate orange sorbet at a dinner, it is because those facts were mentioned somewhere in a letter or journal. The Grimms and their friends did not write their letters and journals in English, of course, so the phrases that you see quoted throughout are translations from the German.

When I mention the distances from the Amtshaus to the castle in Steinau or the steepness of the streets in Marburg, I do so because I have walked them. On a trip to Germany in the spring of 1999, I visited many of the places where the Grimms had lived. Although some spots were bombed during World War II, many remain almost the same as they were in the nineteenth century. The Amtshaus in Steinau houses a museum of Grimm family artifacts, as does the small castle in the center of the village. In Kassel, one can walk through the gardens of Wilhelmshöhe just as Jacob and Wilhelm did. The palace is open for tours, and the home on the Schöneaussicht, where the Grimms relished the view of the Orangery, is now the home of Die Brüder Grimm-Museum. The streets near the university in Marburg are just as steep and narrow as they were when Jacob first climbed them, and the fountain in the Göttingen town square is much as it was when the brothers taught at the university there.

If you want to visit what German tourist agencies call "the fairy tale road" for a virtual tour or to plan your own geographical adventure, you can make a good start on the internet at two Web sites: Kassel (http://www.kassel.de) or Steinau (http://www.main-kinzig.net/steinau/).

THE GRIMMS IN THEIR OWN WORDS

While there are many sources for Jacob and Wilhelm's own words, many are in German. Both brothers wrote brief autobiographies that talk about their lives through the mid-1820s. They are combined in *Die Brüder Grimm in ihren Selbstbiographien*, ed. Manfred Kluge (Munich: Wilhelm Heyne, 1985).

A German scholar named Wilhelm Schoof has published many collections of the Grimms' letters, including: *Briefe der Brüder Grimm an Savigny*, co-edited with Ingeborg Schnack (Berlin: Erich Schmidt, 1953) and *Briefwechsel Zwischen Jacob und Wilhelm Grimm aus der Jugenzeit* (Weimar: Herman Böhlaus, 1963).

Jacob's first impressions of life at the university in Marburg appear in his letters to Paul Wigand: *Briefe der Brüder Grimm an Paul Wigand*, ed. E. Stengel (Marburg: N. G. Elsert'sche, 1910).

A striking history of the Grimms in their own words was published in three volumes in celebration of the two hundredth anniversary of their births. The first volume has material about their personal lives and their writing; the second deals with their brother Ludwig; the third, produced in two parts, presented the brothers in the context of the politics of their times: *Die Brüder Grimm: Dokumente ihres Lebens und Wirkens*, eds. Dieter Hennig and Bernhard Lauer, vol. I; *Ludwig Emil Grimm 1790–1863: Maler, Zeichner, Radierer*, eds. Ingrid Koszinowski and Vera Leuschner, vol. II; *Die Brüder Grimm in ihrer amtlichen und politischen Tätigkeit: Ausstellungskatalog*, eds. Hans Bernd Harder and Ekkehard Kaufmann, vol. III, part 1; *Die Brüder Grimm in ihrer amtlichen und politischen Tätigkeit: Aufsätze*, eds. Hans Bernd Harder and Ekkehard Kaufmann, vol. III, part 2 (Kassel: Weber and Weidemeyer, 1985–1986).

TALES AND LEGENDS

While there are hundreds of editions of the *Household Tales*, the best translation and edition is Jack Zipes's *The Complete Fairy Tales of the*

Brothers Grimm (New York: Bantam Books, 1987). Zipes includes the tales that the Grimms had deleted and provides details on sources of the individual stories.

The legends have been translated by Donald Ward in *The German Legends of the Brothers Grimm,* 2 vols. (Philadelphia: Institute for the Study of Human Issues, 1981).

OTHER BIOGRAPHIES

All of the following books are out of print and not available in bookstores, but you might be able to find them at your public library. I did and discovered that each of them emphasizes rather different aspects of the brothers' lives: Muriel Hammond, *Jacob and Wilhelm Grimm: The Fairy-Tale Brothers* (London: Dobson Books, 1968); Ruth Michaelis-Jena, *The Brothers Grimm* (New York: Praeger, 1970); Murray Peppard, *Paths Through the Forest* (New York: Holt, Rinehart, and Winston, 1971); Robert Quackenbush, *Once Upon a Time: A Story of the Brothers Grimm* (Englewood Cliffs, New Jersey: Prentice-Hall, 1985).

THEIR LIVES IN ART

Ludwig Grimm gives us fascinating views of Germany and the Grimms in his sketches, paintings, and etchings. A good collection appears in Ingrid Koszinowski's *Ludwig Emil Grimm: Zeichnungen und Gemälde,* 2 vols. (Marburg: Hitzeroth, 1990).

LIFE IN FRANCE AND GERMANY

There are thousands of books about the French Revolution, but one that recorded the impressions of a soldier from the Grimms' province is particularly interesting: Jakob Walter's *The Diary of a Napoleonic Foot Soldier,* ed. Marc Raeff (New York: Doubleday, 1991).

A Few Words About Sources

When I wanted background information on Germany, I turned to Martin Kitchen's *The Cambridge Illustrated History of Germany* (Cambridge: Cambridge University Press, 1996).

Complete List of Tales

Story titles from *The Complete Fairy Tales of the Brothers Grimm,* translated and
edited by Jack Zipes. New York: Bantam Books, 1987.

COMPLETE LIST OF TALES

The Seven Ravens
Simple Hans*
The Singing Bone
The Six Swans
Snow White
The Sparrow and His Four Children
The Star Coins
The Stepmother*
The Stolen Pennies
The Strange Feast**
The Straw, the Coal, and the Bean
Sweetheart Roland
The Tablecloth, the Knapsack, the Cannon
    Hat, and the Horn*
A Tale About the Boy Who Went Forth to
    Learn What Fear Was
The Three Feathers
The Three Little Gnomes in the Forest
The Three Sisters*
The Three Spinners
Thumbling's Travels
The Twelve Brothers
The Twelve Huntsmen
The Virgin Mary's Child
The Water Nixie
The Wedding of Mrs. Fox
The White Snake
The Wolf and the Seven Young Kids

TALES ADDED IN VOLUME TWO OF
CHILDREN'S AND HOUSEHOLD TALES (1815)

The Animals of the Lord and the Devil
The Beam
Bearskin
The Blue Light
The Bright Sun Will Bring It to Light
The Children of Famine*
The Clever Farmer's Daughter
The Clever Little Tailor
The Crows***
The Devil and His Grandmother
The Devil's Sooty Brother
Doctor Know-It-All

The Domestic Servants
The Donkey
The Expert Huntsman
The Faithful Animals†
Faithful Ferdinand and Unfaithful
    Ferdinand
The Fleshing Flail from Heaven
The Fox and the Horse
The Gnome
The Golden Key
The Goose Girl
Hans My Hedgehog
The Iron Stove
The Jew in the Thornbush
The King of the Golden Mountain
Knoist and His Three Sons
The Lazy One and the Industrious One*
The Lazy Spinner
The Lion and the Frog*
The Little Lamb and the Little Fish
The Little Shroud
The Long Nose*
The Maiden from Brakel
The Old Beggar Woman
The Old Woman in the Forest
The Poor Man and the Rich Man
The Poor Miller's Apprentice and the Cat
Pretty Katrinelya and Pif Paf Poltree
The Raven
The Rejuvenated Little Old Man
Saint Solicitous*
Simelei Mountain
The Singing, Springing Lark
The Six Servants
The Soldier and the Carpenter*
The Spirit in the Glass Bottle
The Stubborn Child
The Sweet Porridge
The Tale About the Land of Cockaigne
Tales About Toads
A Tale with a Riddle
A Tall Tale from Ditmarsh
The Three Army Surgeons
The Three Black Princesses
The Three Brothers

Complete List of Tales

The Three Journeymen
The Three Lazy Sons
The Three Little Birds
The Turnip
The Two Kings' Children
The Ungrateful Son
The Water of Life
The White Bride and the Black Bride
The Wild Man****
The Worn-out Dancing Shoes
The Wren and the Bear
The Young Giant

TALES ADDED IN THE SECOND EDITION OF
CHILDREN'S AND HOUSEHOLD TALES (1819)

The Blessed Virgin's Little Glass
The Bremen Town Musicians
Brother Lustig
Choosing a Bride
Clever Else
Clever Gretel
The Devil with the Three Golden Hairs
Faithful Johannes
The Four Skillful Brothers
The Fox and His Cousin
The Fox and the Cat
Freddy and Katy
Gambling Hans
God's Food
Going Traveling
The Good Bargain
Hans Gets Married
The Hare's Bride
The Hazel Branch
The Heavenly Wedding
How Six Made Their Way in the World
The Knapsack, the Hat, and the Horn
The Leftovers
The Lettuce Donkey
The Little Old Lady
The Little Shepherd Boy
Lucky Hans
The Marvelous Minstrel

Old Hildebrand
One-Eye, Two-Eyes, and Three-Eyes
The Pink Flower
Poverty and Humility Lead to Heaven
The Prince Who Feared Nothing
The Riddle
The Rose
Saint Joseph in the Forest
The Seven Swabians
The Tailor in Heaven
The Thief and His Master
The Three Languages
The Three Snake Leaves
The Three Sons of Fortune
Thumbling
The Twelve Apostles
The Two Brothers
The Wolf and the Fox
The Wolf and the Man

TALES ADDED IN THE THIRD EDITION OF
CHILDREN'S AND HOUSEHOLD TALES (1837)

The Clever Servant
The Glass Coffin
The Griffin
Lazy Heinz
Mother Trudy
The Peasant in Heaven
Snow White and Rose Red
Strong Hans

TALES ADDED IN THE FOURTH EDITION OF
CHILDREN'S AND HOUSEHOLD TALES (1840)

The Bittern and the Hoopoe
The Flounder
The House in the Forest
Lean Lisa
The Life Span
The Messengers of Death
Misfortune ‡
The Owl
Sharing Joys and Sorrows
The Wren

COMPLETE LIST OF TALES

TALES ADDED IN THE FIFTH EDITION OF
CHILDREN'S AND HOUSEHOLD TALES (1843)

The Crumbs on the Table
The Drummer
Eve's Unequal Children
The Giant and the Tailor
The Goose Girl at the Spring
The Hare and the Hedgehog
Master Pfreim
The Master Thief
The Nail
The Nixie in the Pond
The Pea Test †
The Peasant and the Devil
The Poor Boy in the Grave
The Robber and His Sons ‡
Spindle, Shuttle, and Needle
The True Bride
The Two Travelers

TALES ADDED IN THE SIXTH EDITION OF
CHILDREN'S AND HOUSEHOLD TALES (1850)

The Boots of Buffalo Leather
The Crystal Ball
The Ear of Corn
The Gifts of the Little Folk
The Grave Mound
Iron Hans
Maid Maleen
Old Rinkrank

TALES ADDED IN THE SEVENTH EDITION OF
CHILDREN'S AND HOUSEHOLD TALES (1857)

The Clever People
The Little Hamster from the Water
The Moon
The Twelve Lazy Servants

*Omitted beginning with the 1819 edition.
**Omitted beginning with the 1837 edition.
***Omitted beginning with the 1840 edition.
****Omitted beginning with the 1843 edition.
†Omitted beginning with the 1850 edition.
‡Omitted beginning with the 1857 edition.
§ Moved to the notes of the 1822 volume.

Picture Credits

Brüder Grimm-Museum, Kassel: pp. 7, 13, 40, 56, 86, 107, 114, 117, 121

Museum Hanau, Schloss Philippsruhe, Bildstelle Hanau: pp. 11, 25, 43, 98, 104, 108 (left and right), 109, 134, 138

Hekman Library, Calvin College: frontispiece

Hessisches Staatsarchiv, Marburg: p. 80

Donald R. Hettinga: pp. 6 (bottom), 9

Zane T. Hettinga: p. 6 (top)

Paintings by Michael Hofman, Germanishes Nationalmuseum, Nürnberg: p. 143

Painting by Ludwig Strack: p. 26

Painting by G. K. Urlaub. Verwaltung der Staatlichen Schlösser und Gärten Hessen, Bad Homberg: p. 16

Verwaltung der Staatlichen Schlösser und Gärten Hessen, Bad Homberg: pp. 2, 12, 14 (top and bottom), 16, 34, 87, 105, 106, 113, 126

Engraving by A. G. Vickers. Hekman Library, Calvin College: p. 133

Timeline

Year	The Brothers Grimm
1783	
1785	Jacob born, January 4
1786	Wilhelm born, February 24
1788	
1791	Grimms move to Steinau
1793	
1796	Their father dies
1798	Brothers go away to school in Kassel
1799	
1800	
1802	Jacob goes to the University of Marburg
1803	Wilhelm goes to the University of Marburg
1805	
1806	Jacob Secretary of the Hessian War College
1808	Their mother dies; Jacob Librarian to King Jérôme Bonaparte
1809	
1812	Volume I of *Household Tales* published
1814	Wilhelm Secretary to the Librarian in Kassel; Jacob in Paris and Vienna
1815	Volume II of *Household Tales* published
1816	Part I of *German Legends* published
1818	Part II of *German Legends* published
1819	Jacob: *German Grammar,* Volume I

	World Events
	American Revolution ends
	U.S. Constitution
	King Louis XVI of France executed by guillotine
	George Washington dies
	Alessandro Volta produces electricity from the first battery
	The city of Chicago begins as Fort Dearborn
	Lewis & Clark make the first crossing of North America
	Holy Roman Empire collapses
	Beethoven writes Symphony no. 5
	Abraham Lincoln born
	U.S. declares war on Great Britain
	British troops burn the White House
	Sir David Brewster invents the kaleidoscope
	Mary Shelley publishes *Frankenstein*

Year	The Brothers Grimm
1825	Wilhelm marries Dorothea Wild
1828	Herman Grimm born
1829	Wilhelm: *German Heroic Tales*
1830	Positions at the University of Göttingen
1831	
1833	Lotte Grimm dies
1836	
1837	Protest of the Göttingen Seven
1840	Brothers called to Berlin
1841	Brothers move to Berlin
1843	Jacob travels to Italy
1844	Jacob travels to Sweden
1845	Hans Christian Andersen visits
1847	
1848	Jacob a representative in Frankfurt parliament
1849	
1851	Jacob: *On the Origin of Language;* Wilhelm: *On the History of Rhyme*
1854	Volume I of *German Dictionary* published
1855	
1857	
1859	Wilhelm dies, December 16
1860	Volume II of *German Dictionary* published
1863	Jacob dies, September 20

World Events

Noah Webster publishes *An American Dictionary of English*

Emily Dickinson born

Charles Darwin sails to South America

Battle of the Alamo in Texas; Davy Crockett killed

Samuel Morse invents the telegraph

Composer Peter Ilich Tchaikovsky dies

Scotsman James Braid discovers hypnosis

Charles Dickens publishes *A Christmas Carol*

Frederick Douglass publishes his autobiography;
Henry David Thoreau moves into a hut on Walden Pond

Thomas Edison is born

Gold rush at Sutter's Mill

Harriet Tubman escapes a Maryland plantation

Herman Melville publishes *Moby-Dick*

Walt Whitman publishes *Leaves of Grass*

Louis Pasteur proves fermentation caused by bacteria

Abraham Lincoln elected president

South Carolina secedes from Union

Index

Page numbers in **bold** type refer to illustrations.

Index

Index

Index